1979

The Teaching of Pronunciation

The Teaching of Pronunciation

Peter MacCarthy

M.A. Cantab.

Former Head of the Phonetics Department
University of Leeds

Cambridge University Press
Cambridge
London · New York · Melbourne

Published by the Syndics of the Cambridge University Press
The Pitt Building, Trumpington Street, Cambridge CB2 1RP
Bentley House, 200 Euston Road, London NW1 2DB
32 East 57th Street, New York, NY 10022, USA
296 Beaconsfield Parade, Middle Park, Melbourne 3206, Australia

First published 1978

Printed in Great Britain at the
University Press, Cambridge

Library of Congress Cataloguing in Publication Data

MacCarthy, Peter Arthur Desmond.

The teaching of pronunciation.

Bibliography: p.
1. Language and languages – Study and teaching.
2. English language – Study and teaching – Foreign students.
3. English language – Pronunciation – Study and teaching.
4. Phonetics. I. Title.
P53.M217   418.′007   77–84809
ISBN 0 521 21852 7

Contents

418.007
M131

87595

v

vi

Introduction

It is hoped that this book will interest any who teach, or might teach, a spoken language to those for whom it is a 'foreign' language, i.e. not the mother tongue. It is designed to be of practical use to them in their task.

Though a certain amount of factual information is to be found in these pages, the book is not primarily concerned to set out the facts about particular languages, to provide a phonetic description of them. Books have already been written and others will doubtless yet be written with that aim, seeking either to bring to light what has not so far been described or adequately described, or perhaps to present differently what is already known.

In this book attention is concentrated mainly on persons: on speakers of languages and on learners of languages; and my words are addressed in the first place to the teachers of languages, especially those who engage in assisting people to speak a language not their own – whether or not it be the mother tongue of the teacher. I have attempted in Part 1 to put down some rather general thoughts for consideration and then, in Part 2, to set the subject of pronunciation, as I see it, in its place alongside other branches of language and of language study. In Parts 3 and 4 the principal tendencies of learners of various nationalities are described in broad outline. Those who are engaged in the teaching of English will see Part 4 as directed primarily to them; those teaching other languages to speakers of English will go rather to Part 3. I would however suggest that an interest of both categories of teachers in the converse Part will not be found unprofitable: not only will they be preparing themselves for occupying as teachers the reciprocal role at any time, but they may well gain some fresh insights into their habitual one.

When dealing with techniques and procedures of pronunciation teaching, in as much detail as seemed appropriate, I have constantly drawn on personal experience, on my memories of those who taught me, and my recollections of colleagues and of students: from all of them, and from my own efforts, I have learnt and continue to learn a great deal about how not to do things besides, as I believe, how to do them. I hope that my conclusions are broadly sound, for it would bring me great satisfaction to feel I had been able to pass on to others something that I personally consider important and that they could turn to good account in their own teaching, besides perhaps saving them some time and trouble in their daily work.

Finally, I would urge those who read this book to take every opportunity that presents itself for obtaining some of the practical training that no book can give. In turn, I now look hopefully for extended provision of such courses of practical training in phonetics, for which present need is great and of which far too few are available.

1 Teaching

1.1 Teaching and learning

Successful teaching means having succeeded in creating conditions in which learning takes place. To aim at effective teaching means to try to achieve conditions – within limitations imposed by the situation in which the teacher finds himself – in which effective learning occurs. (Throughout this book, 'teacher' = person doing the teaching, master, mistress, lecturer, instructor; and 'learner' = a person being taught, pupil, student. The reader will be able to supply whichever term is most appropriate and to read 'she, her' for 'he, him' etc. as necessary.)

Much teaching is carried out by word of mouth – orally, and the learner then learns through listening – aurally. Teaching can also be conducted through some form of writing; this book has been written in the hope that, in reading it, somebody will learn something. At times, both oral and written instruction can usefully be supported visually by pictures and diagrams in books and by drawing or writing on a blackboard. In the pages that follow, our attention will be directed mainly towards oral teaching to an individual or to the individuals of whom every group consists.

1.2 Learning facts and learning skills

There is a major distinction to be made between the learning of facts and the learning of skills – though many teaching situations involve some combination of both. If you tell a person *about* something, you are giving out information, imparting factual knowledge with respect to that thing. Learning can be said to have taken place when the receiver of the information grasps the sense of what is said, remembers it for the future, and is able to reproduce it in some suitable form as and when required. So here comprehension and memory are the faculties that are concerned and that need to be cultivated.

Some of the factors that can contribute to the success or otherwise of the processes involved in this type of learning are: the clarity of the description or explanation that is given; the choice of words, adapted to the age and degree of maturity or sophistication of the learner; the order of presentation and the grading of material, with the elementary preceding and leading to the more advanced. This kind of thing affects not only initial grasp of the basic meaning and appreciation of the full significance of what is said, but also its retention.

In dealing with such matters, it is well that the teacher should keep a clear picture before him of the *purpose* of what he is doing. This will help in making the best choice between courses of action open to him and give direction and coherence to the teaching, which will in turn promote effective learning. It is not of course necessary, or in most cases desirable, that the learner should have all this explained to him: whether or not to 'take him behind the scenes' has to be decided by each teacher in the light of all the circumstances – in particular, of the learner's degree of maturity, and of the time available.

The learning of skills is quite another thing. Here, the ability to perform specific actions consisting usually of complex and precisely co-ordinated movements is what has to be cultivated, and this needs developing to the point where the actions become habitual through much rehearsal and repetition so that they get carried out automatically and unconsciously, in the exact form required.

The foregoing general description could apply to learning to swim, learning to play the piano, or learning to speak a language. Appropriate techniques for each will be available to a teacher provided they have already been worked out; if not, he may have to invent them as he goes along. Of course many skills, including those just mentioned, can be 'picked up' without a teacher; but the point is that the desired level of attainment would very likely not be reached without outside guidance, faulty habits may be acquired, much time could be wasted, efficiency suffers.

So, the guidance of a teacher may take the form of putting into operation certain techniques and procedures, or may consist of imparting relevant information. It is always up to the teacher to judge what form the guidance should take and at what point in time it is best given.

1.3   Motivation

One of the essential conditions for effective learning has to do with motivation. Sometimes teaching is conducted against a background of lack of motivation, but since it is certain that little effective learning takes place when motivation is poor, it is vital that the teacher should do everything possible to promote good, strong motivation and do nothing that might inhibit it.

Some powerful sources of motivation are already present in the situation and do not derive from the teacher: motives that spring to mind are, for instance, the desire to reach a given standard, perhaps to pass some examination or test, or to gain a qualification leading to an advantageous position or career. Again, individuals vary as to what acts as an incentive to learning in their particular case: some people are driven to excel, they are keen to be good at whatever they turn their hand to; for them it is a matter of personal pride and self-esteem, which would suffer if they were to permit themselves to fall short of the highest standard, or of the standard they know themselves to be capable of. Others feel the urge to do better than their fellows; in them the competitive spirit is strong, they obtain their personal satisfaction from the sense of their relative superiority, and the recognition by others of that superiority. Others again are appreciative of approval, whether from their fellows or from higher authority; they get discouraged if approval is withheld, or resentful should disapproval be incurred. Most of us experience all these feelings at different times and in varying degree.

Those who seem to have *no* strong incentive can be a problem to their teachers, whose task it will be to look for all possible means to stimulate their interest and a desire to learn. By treating learners as individuals a teacher will in time get to know what each is like, what he responds favourably to, which type of approach is likely to be counter-productive; in his teaching he will be guided accordingly.

1.4 The teacher as speaker

Among the external conditions influencing the learning, those that stem directly from the teacher, many of which are under his control, are undoubtedly the most important. His own performance *as a speaker* is of the utmost significance. For a start, it is a well-known fact that countless audiences get addressed by speakers who just cannot be heard much beyond the front row. Every speaker should set out to address those in the back row; let him then imagine that those in the back row are the only people in the room, when he will of course find himself addressing them automatically. Inaudibility breeds frustration, then inattention, then boredom. Learning cannot thrive under these conditions.

Actual volume of sound apart, inattention and boredom are liable to set in when the effect on the listener is of insufficient variety. This may be lack of variety in *pitch* (the intonation is too 'flat', too much like a mono-

3

tone); lack of variety in *volume* itself (with too little emphasis important words may fail to stand out from the less important); lack of variety in *timing* (speeding up and slowing down the rate of speaking should vary with, and be dictated by, the subject matter and by the size and composition of one's audience; and the flow of speech needs to be punctuated by suitable pauses, which should themselves be of varied duration). Any impression of lack of variety, leading to loss of attention and interest, may be due to some combination of the foregoing.

Critical examination of his own vocal equipment, and of the use he makes of it, is therefore recommended to every lecturer and classroom teacher. In a few cases expert help is needed if he is to avoid damaging his voice, maybe permanently. In many more cases advice and perhaps some training is required if a speaker is to be audible to the whole of his audience and maximally effective as a teacher.

To conclude by considering a wider range of personal attributes: the teacher's whole behaviour, his reactions and responses, the attitudes he adopts, the personality he exhibits and the overall effect he creates, determine – more than any kind of expertise or mastery of a subject or a method – his ultimate effectiveness as a teacher. Qualities of patience and tolerance, consideration and tact; interest shown in the matter in hand, and in the individual learner; attention to detail, insistence on high standards of accuracy; even the ability to make a joke or to enjoy one – but not at someone's expense (unless it be at one's own!) – these are some of the character traits that would be held desirable in most walks of life, that we each of us possess in varying measure and as teachers should surely seek to cultivate.

1.5 Some external factors affecting learning

It is often not realised how much various other external factors can affect adversely the concentration and interest that should be brought to every learning situation. If the adverse factors are under the control of the teacher – some of course are not – he should see to their removal, and should be ever on the look-out for things of this nature. Background noise should be eliminated wherever possible, doors and windows closed to unwanted sound from outside – unless conditions of temperature and ventilation would deteriorate too greatly as a result. Noise generated within the room need not be tolerated: a creaky seat can often be exchanged for another, the shuffling of feet, the rustling of paper and casual conversation can and should be discouraged. A fidgety audience is generally one whose attention is not being held – let every teacher and

4

public speaker take note! However, it has to be accepted that the very young do have great difficulty in keeping still for any length of time, and any movement is liable to produce noise. Then the acoustic properties of a room may be at fault: most teaching spaces are too reverberant, amplifying all sound unduly. If the level of unwanted sound is excessive – and a sensitive teacher will notice when it is – this in itself can make speaking and listening fatiguing and thus render effective teaching and learning in some cases almost impossible. Sound-absorbent treatment of walls and ceiling, and perhaps some floor covering, would effect an enormous improvement, so this should be considered and carried out if at all feasible – as it sometimes is. Absorbent material can perhaps be fixed to the ceiling and/or some of the walls of a classroom. Anything that will break up smooth hard surfaces is good: 'egg-boxes' work wonders, cost little or nothing, and the result is not too unsightly.

Visual considerations should not be overlooked. There should of course be adequate light shed on everything that has to be looked at: the teacher himself, the notes he needs to consult, the book he reads from, the blackboard, the learner, the learner's writing surface, and so forth. What is written up on the blackboard should not be too small or too faint. The board itself should be cleared of unwanted material as soon as much has accumulated on it.

Some people find themselves at a disadvantage compared to others owing to their position in a room in relation to the teacher. For most oral work it is desirable that teacher and learner should be able to see each other. One or other ought therefore to shift so that a larger person, say, does not interfere with the line of vision between the teacher and a smaller person sitting just behind. Those with any marked hearing disability or with poor eyesight should be encouraged to sit near the front, if they have not already taken up their position there. No one should have to sit in an unpleasant draught or too near a hot radiator, or with a bright light shining in his eye. Seating need not be luxurious but it ought not to be positively uncomfortable, which it can become after a certain length of time.

It is not pampering on the part of a teacher to give thought to such things and to remedy what lies in his power. It is all part of the general aim: to ensure favourable conditions for good learning to take place.

2 Teaching pronunciation

The teaching of pronunciation must first be considered in the wider context of learning a language. Now not only is a language a complex thing, but language activity can take a variety of forms. There can be few people learning a foreign language who do not wish eventually to become proficient in a number of these activities, of which the most basic are: hearing, speaking, reading and writing.

2.1 Language and speech

Reception and performance

Hearing and reading are receptive activities: you receive the message that is being conveyed by means of language, in the first case through apprehending by ear what has been spoken, and in the second through apprehending by eye what has been put into written form.

Speaking and writing are performing activities: you send the message to be conveyed, in the one case by movements of your own speech organs to produce sounds that pass from your mouth, through air, to the ear and so to the brain of a receiving person – normally another person but inevitably also, and conceivably only, yourself. In the case of writing, your activity consists in putting marks on a surface, whether by pen on paper, chalk on blackboard, or by means of a machine such as a typewriter.

Speech and writing

The language, or languages, stored in a person's mind can be made to materialise through the medium of speech or through that of writing ('writing' here covers what has been written by hand as well as more sophisticated forms such as typed and printed matter). Using the medium of speech, the performer is tied to the time dimension and performs, as it were, on the time track, and when his performance is at an end there is nothing to show for it – though its effects can remain in someone's memory. (A modern exception to this would of course be any kind of recording of the performance.) With the medium of writing, its actual execution is equally tied to the time dimension, but the written marks that remain are independent of time – or place, provided they can be transported elsewhere: books and letters are intended to be moved around whereas what is written on a blackboard generally stays there until rubbed out.

The activities of hearing and speaking are concerned with spoken language or speech; those of reading and writing are concerned with written language (handwriting, print, typescript). The activity of reading aloud exceptionally involves both.

With spoken language, the speaking activity is never involved alone, always the hearing activity is involved as well – even if there is no other listener *as you speak you hear yourself*. Exceptions would be supposing the speaker is stone deaf, or when 'talking in one's sleep' – though hearing of a sort presumably can take place since it is possible to wake oneself up by sounds one has uttered while asleep.

Speaking and pronouncing

Speaking and pronouncing both relate to the same basic activity but pronouncing concentrates on *how* the speaking is done; though speaking necessarily involves pronouncing, a consideration of speaking takes into account also *what* is said, the ideas expressed, the words used, the constructions and turns of phrase, the style and so forth.

It is possible to know a language well without opening one's mouth. All the other activities can be carried on perfectly satisfactorily: the language can be understood when it is heard spoken, it can be read and understood from a written text, it is possible for it to be written down correctly, effectively and in impeccable style – all by a person who has not spoken a word, and even supposing he were unable to do so. But to be in a position to speak a language well, you have to know what are suitable things to say in a given situation and know the words that will express them; then at every moment you have to find the words you need for what you want to say, having regard to all the circumstances. You have in some way to call up bits of the language from your inner consciousness and order these mentally in a suitable sequence so that instructions from the brain reach your breathing and articulating mechanisms in the form that will enable them to go into action and produce the required succession of sounds smoothly, rapidly but with appropriate variations of pace, and grouped according to sense with the right amount of stopping and slowing at specific points.

Speaking a language, then, clearly involves more than just pronouncing it. But one could pronounce a language well and know or use relatively few words and phrases of it; one could pronounce a language well and still be quite unable to converse in it, or express oneself adequately in it, or discourse on certain topics while using it. And one could be capable of pronouncing a language well but when the occasion arises for using it be unable to find the words to match the situation, or only find them, and so utter them, slowly and with unwanted hesitations.

It will be seen that the answers to: Do you know (English)?; Do you speak (English)?; How well do you know (can you speak) the language? can be very different – though the questioner may have framed his inquiry under the impression that questions such as the above all amount to the same thing.

2.2 Why pronounce well?

Before going into problems of actually teaching the pronunciation of a foreign language, let us examine the attitude that can be summarised by the question: *why* have a good pronunciation? – whether the attitude, on the part of teacher or taught, be put into words or not.

With so much more attention being paid nowadays to spoken as distinct from written language – compared to what was formerly the case, with almost complete neglect of the speaking side – it is now usual to find wide acknowledgement of the importance of *speaking* a foreign language well, in the sense at least of communicating by word of mouth with other people through its use. But it needs to be realised that the act of communication itself is interfered with or made more difficult, to an extent often not appreciated, when the *manner* of communicating is at fault. The extreme, but quite common, case is where comprehension of the (correctly formed) message to be conveyed is not achieved – in other words, communication simply fails to take place. Then there is the stage when the basic sense of a message does get through, but communication is slow, partial or delayed. Everyone knows, too, how it is often possible to get out of some awkward situation when attempts at a spoken language not one's own are proving inadequate, by recourse to expressive gesticulation, by hopefully resorting to one's mother tongue, by drawing pictures, or by looking round for an interpreter. But of course none of these ways of dealing with a problem of communication involve handling another person's – the receiver's – language, one foreign to the speaker. And none of the levels of performance implied in the foregoing could possibly be accepted as a proper standard to aim at in any programme of teaching a foreign language.

Let us now consider the matter from the opposite point of view, that of the effect created on a hearer by one's actually pronouncing his language in one way rather than another. This is partly an aesthetic matter for the individual, partly a social matter. There is no doubt that people have views on the subject of how their language *should* be spoken, how they like to hear it spoken – particularly by foreigners. Now although some of these views could be called naive, irrational or misguided, it would be unwise for the learner to disregard them entirely: subconscious attitudes unfavourable to the foreign speaker can be due to no more than something about his 'way of speaking'. These attitudes may take forms such as impatience at undue hesitation or slowness; dislike (for whatever reason) of some particular mispronunciation that begins to irritate when it keeps recurring; a sense of lack of sympathy or intimacy or deeper understanding because of a pervasive impression of strangeness; or just the vague feeling that the speaker could, if he had wished, have taken greater trouble to pronounce one's language well, which is then felt to show a certain want of regard for the language and thus, in a sense, perhaps for oneself.

Now clearly, at the level of casual encounters with strangers in shop or street a person may not much care what impression he creates and indeed it cannot matter a great deal – apart from considerations of common courtesy. It is in situations where personal relationships can develop, views can be exchanged and viewpoints appreciated, that *manner* of speaking can make a difference. The favourable effect of a good pronunciation can include absence of distraction from the subject matter in hand, leading to more effective and satisfactory communication; the agreeable feeling that, after all, not so much divides people of differing linguistic backgrounds as one had perhaps thought; even some awareness that care and trouble must have been taken to reach such a standard in another language, which – it being the listener's own – can only be gratifying to him. In any case, the result is likely to be more rather than less friendliness all round – which means in the end an improvement, however small, in the relationships between people.

It is very desirable that a language teacher be able to put into words reasons why good pronunciation should be aimed at, if the point is ever raised by his pupils. It is even more desirable that he himself be firmly convinced of the importance of good pronunciation, and that this should at all times emerge implicitly from the mere fact that he pays attention to their pronunciation, notices mistakes and takes time and trouble to put them right. But of this more in greater detail later. The reasons just advanced for *having* a good pronunciation take into account none of the beneficial effects of *working* at improving one's pronunciation of a language: there is much of general educational and psychological value in the self-knowledge that is gained by all, and in the efforts at self-mastery that are demanded, in trying to achieve a high standard of performance in a foreign tongue.

Foreign residence

At this point it is necessary to dispose of a common fallacy found even – perhaps particularly – among those who think that pronunciation is indeed important: the idea that how to pronounce well need not be taught because all will come right as soon as the learner spends a period of time among native speakers of the language, preferably in a country where it is in use. Now residence in a country is of inestimable value for acquiring its language, even for 'speaking' it, but by no means inevitably or automatically for *pronouncing* it. To rely on foreign residence alone for good pronunciation is inefficient and time-wasting – indeed, one can wait a lifetime without achieving a respectable standard: we all know of foreigners living permanently in our country who continue indefinitely to betray the characteristic speech habits of their mother tongue. What residence in the country does do is to benefit enormously a number of things *other than* pronunciation: comprehension of a language when spoken, in all its variety, and at speed, by all kinds of speakers; mastery of idiom and vocabulary, and ability to call up promptly the words and phrases for what one wants to say. All these things – besides many others outside language, such as the culture and institutions, the ways of the people, the architecture of their towns and the topography of the countryside – can quite properly be 'picked up', for the most part without explicit instruction and largely subconsciously. (It might be argued that fluency, i.e. the ability to say words and phrases fast enough, is one of the things that is bound to come with the practice that is obtained through much talking in a language. But this kind of fluency is hardly worth having if the very speed with which words are uttered makes them harder to follow – which is what happens when many or even a few of them are pronounced imperfectly.)

The reasons why this does not work with pronunciation are partly to do with the firm habits of the mother tongue coupled with not knowing how to go about putting other habits in their place – the habits appropriate to the foreign language to be learnt; and partly with the failure to *notice* just *how* people actually speak, due to inability to direct the auditory attention to this, which is itself due to *lack of training* in directing the attention and, most probably, insufficient knowledge of proper techniques for such training.

Work in class on a spoken language should be looked upon as essential preparation for any foreign residence that may be planned: work in class can do some things that going abroad in itself cannot do, and it can do other things more efficiently and expeditiously. To go and stay or live in a foreign country inadequately prepared to take advantage of the opportunities this offers is a deplorable waste of time and money, and it is up to the language teacher to see that this wastage as far as possible does not occur.

Here are some of the forms of preparation that will save time and increase efficiency: a teacher can give factual information as and when required; he can point out what needs attention; he can select and demonstrate whatever has to be presented to the learner's ear; he can show how a piece of pronouncing ought to be done, and also how it ought not to be done – in particular how the learner himself is doing it or tends to do it; he can put into execution techniques and procedures for getting effective results, devising his own exercises if necessary or so desired; he can coach, or coax, the performer gradually to achieve a higher and higher standard of performance. More specifically as a preliminary to the time abroad he can, when demonstrating in the early stages, slow up the normal rate of utterance so that the learner can catch the sound, and so grasps some point, before having to cope with more rapid rates and longer stretches of speech, first in the classroom, then abroad; the teacher can see to it that a good model of pronunciation is presented to the listener's ear at all times, and can offer advice as to which of several varieties or alternatives had best be imitated and adopted, wherever a choice matters on social, regional or other grounds. This is the kind of thing that the learner already in a foreign country cannot possibly assess – even supposing he notices the differences – so expert guidance is needed. And even if the non-native teacher (one who speaks natively the language of his pupils and not their target language) cannot be expected to have as sensitive an awareness of subtle implications – whether in language usage or in pronunciation – as the native speaker, he may score over the latter by being freer of prejudices, and he may well be able to express points at issue more accurately than the native mother-tongue speaker. Above all, every teacher can prepare his students to be on the look-out for specific things, to be able to identify at once and with precision *what* they hear when they get abroad. They will then be in a better position to reach, on their own, wise decisions as to what ways of speaking to imitate, and in a better position to imitate them.

It goes without saying, but should perhaps be pointed out, that if the language learner can get abroad at a *very* early age, some of the above forms of deliberate preparation are less indicated – for the simple reason that the speech habits of the mother tongue are not so firmly fixed as they become later and there is a good chance that most of the new habits will be correctly acquired unconsciously. And of course the inhibiting self-consciousness of adolescence will not yet have become such a problem.

Performance standards

The question of what level of performance to aim at, and what to be satisfied with, depends very much on the circumstances. Numerous factors have to be taken into account: the age and level of pupils, the length of the course, the purpose(s) for which the foreign language is ultimately required, the end result to be achieved. But bearing in mind what has been said above on the desirability of a good pronunciation there is no reason why the standard aimed at should not be very high, as high as possible in the circumstances. There is also the difference between speaking and pronouncing. Supposing the course to be short, the general level low, the end result sought not an ambitious one, clearly a high *speaking* standard cannot be expected and should not be aimed at. But that does not keep the *pronunciation* standard necessarily low: the articulation of each vowel and consonant sound of the foreign language, and the handling of the main features of sounds in sequence and of connected speech, really ought to be got right however few words and sentences are ultimately learnt; for all this the standard to be aimed at can well be 'near-native'.

Now a person teaching his own language must be assumed to be a perfect model (barring any marked regionalisms and aside from any purely personal 'speech defects'), so here it will simply be a matter of saying: listen to me, then getting the learner to imitate as accurately as possible and insisting on something pretty close to one's own speech. For the teacher of a language not his own, the position in relation to his class is not really very different. Many a teacher who would not for one moment pass as a native speaker in everyday conversation can provide a thoroughly adequate, even admirable, demonstration model at the level of the word and probably of the sentence. Only an occasional lapse in articulation during rapid speech or, in the higher reaches, some intonation pattern that could not be accepted as authentic, need reveal the non-native, and this is of negligible importance in the general run of teaching situations. It is true that the learner cannot be expected to acquire in class a *better* pronunciation than that of his teacher, but there is no reason why he should not strive for one as good; and if, in advanced level work, an exceptionally gifted individual ever reaches the point where his teacher can help him no further in this particular respect, he (the teacher) can feel well satisfied that he has prepared his pupil for taking advantage of everything that foreign residence will be able to add by way of a final polish to an outstanding performance.

Now inevitably, it will as a rule be necessary to settle for something less than perfection, sometimes far less, but the aim can always be high; the decision what to be content with must vary with each case.

Those teachers who are aware of shortcomings in their own performance may, rather naturally, be tempted to dwell less on the pronunciation side in their practical teaching; but if their general approach to pronunciation is similar to that sketched above, they will not rest content but will work to remedy their own deficiencies by all possible means.

2.3   The education of the ear

To leave pronunciation to take care of itself is virtually to ensure that a really acceptable standard is never reached – save possibly by a quite exceptional individual. Those with a certain amount of natural ability, who may well make a favourable impression with the way of speaking that they have been able to 'pick up', are the very ones who stand to profit most from better opportunities if these are made available to them: they can improve so much, and find it so easy to do so, when the relevant plain facts are put before them, if their inadequacies and weaknesses are just pointed out, and if they are made aware of their teacher's concern for a high standard in this domain too – alongside spelling, grammar and all those branches of language study where an almost faultless result is aimed at as a matter of course.

But it follows that if pronunciation is *not* left to take care of itself, whatever one does about it *takes up time*. Now this should not be made the excuse for doing nothing – as it unfortunately often is – but since time is always in short supply in teaching situations, its efficient use is of the utmost importance. In the average language teaching/learning situation, with every branch demanding attention, naturally pronunciation competes with all the rest for time, and to claim for it more than a fair share would be unrealistic. It will fall to each teacher to decide what is the proper share for pronunciation, taking everything into account; but the point needs to be emphasised that *some* time will obviously have to be given to pronunciation if pronunciation is to get any attention at all, and clearly that time should be used as effectively as possible.

Now it has to be accepted that a great deal of what anyone is told about anything 'goes in at one ear and out at the other'. Every teacher knows how most things have to be repeated over and over again before they sink in, and many more times until really learnt – hence all the recapitulation and revision that are normally found unavoidable. Repetition must be accepted as necessary to the learning process, and wherever forgetfulness or the inability to take in something that has been said is due to the mere fact of its not having been heard often enough, repetition is of course just what is needed. But there is a difference between the assimilation of facts or the grasping of explanations and reasoned arguments on the one hand and, on the other, the assimilation of auditory phenomena as such, for which a clear mental picture has got to be established before they can be recalled, and so reproduced. It can happen that facts or arguments are taken in without much need for repetition; this will depend on intellectual development, motivation and many other factors. But where auditory phenomena are concerned, sufficient repetition is the only way to ensure their retention.

We come now to the crucial distinction between learning the mother tongue initially and learning another language at a later date: any other language must be 'superimposed' on the mother tongue, which is already there in the mind and can never be obliterated. Moreover the mother tongue, learnt when the biological motivation for acquiring the basic means of communication with one's environment is at its strongest, has dictated that whatever it contains that is found to assist in the communication process is held on to, whereas whatever is found to be irrelevant to that process is soon disregarded and thereafter given no attention, i.e. is simply not noticed by the hearer. In this way each individual is conditioned by his mother-tongue experience to react in terms of its specific phonological structure. This creates problems as soon as he is required to react differently when confronted with the different phonological structure of his first – or any subsequent – foreign language. (Mother-tongue interference is evident at every level, not only phonetic and phonological of course but syntactic and semantic as well.) Systematic de-conditioning – which in the nature of things can only be partial, never complete – must be embarked upon for its own sake before any new system(s) can be effectively mastered. This represents the most economical use of time: to proceed in any other way takes up, and therefore wastes, so much time as to be not worth considering.

The education of the ear, then, is a prerequisite for efficient foreign language study. For an explanation of the disappointing results commonly reported on language teaching, by whatever 'method', one need look no farther than to the fact that the capacity of the ordinary person to perceive auditorily the phenomena of the language to be learnt is widely, but quite wrongly, taken for granted! Conversely, the whole of language teaching cannot fail to benefit if each learner has been made more aware of linguistic phenomena generally and is better able to recognise and identify them quickly, confidently and reliably when perceived through his own ears. For this a course of training is required.

Principles of auditory training

For any scheme of auditory training to be effective and economical of time the following points need to be borne in mind:

1 The aim is to *train people to listen*, which means paying attention to sounds heard and noticing things about them. There is nothing wrong with people's hearing as such (apart from known disabilities in individual cases): the problem is to learn to direct the attention and the only way to get better at this is to *have practice at doing it*. So the teacher's role here is to provide the opportunities which would otherwise not occur – or only intermittently and in quite haphazard fashion.

2 Listening in order to observe is quite different from listening for comprehension, which is the only type of listening that gets any systematic practice as a rule, whether in mother-tongue acquisition or when foreign language study is begun. Comprehension, which must ultimately come, is achieved more efficiently *after* preparation of the kind here outlined.

3 The technique of directing the attention consists of first making clear, with adequate demonstration, exactly *what* is to be listened for; then giving sufficient, which means a large number of, opportunities of listening for that specific thing, so that each individual can exercise his personal judgment on the audible stimuli presented to him; and finally supplying the correct answers so that each listener can check at once whether his judgment was correct and has therefore to that extent proved itself reliable, or whether any areas of doubt or positive error are revealed, of which he might well have been and have remained unaware, showing the need for further training.

4 Since the aim is to train, not to test, the material should be well within the capacity of everyone present – or almost everyone – to respond to virtually faultlessly. This is one of those activities where there is little point in establishing who can do better than someone else: each person can derive benefit from exercising his auditory judgment and gain confidence and reassurance from discovering the extent of his powers of recognition, identification and discrimination when his concentration has been brought to bear. Until one has actually tried listening for a given distinction, one simply does not know whether one can recognise it consistently, and so trust one's own judgment, or not. People usually

imagine they perform in this domain with a higher standard of accuracy than is in fact the case, and there is a widespread tendency to take far too much for granted. Moreover, when one is confronted with *unfamiliar* auditory effects the judgment commonly becomes strikingly unreliable, even to the extent of thinking one hears differences where none exist.

5 At the outset of foreign language study – or as soon as possible thereafter – the psychological approach to language in general can be most rewardingly broadened, and the hitherto total dependence on the mother-tongue experience advantageously reduced, if the learner can develop some kind of perceptual framework within which to locate and relate audible language phenomena in general. He can do this through being deliberately helped to awareness of the distinct and separate parameters or scales along which auditory effects are capable of varying. These parameters should be presented singly before they appear together – as they invariably do in natural languages. This means that the material used should not be taken from any actual language since that would inevitably be much too complex for presentation in the first instance. Instead, all the early work should be on these basic parameters of speech, which operate or are likely to operate in almost any language. Practice at responding in terms of them helps to establish that perceptual framework into which all languages can subsequently be fitted, and prepares the learner of a foreign language to accept and handle appropriately the phenomena proper to it. The intention is at the same time to bring about some degree of de-conditioning from that mother-tongue influence which otherwise leads a learner to interpret linguistic events automatically and exclusively in terms of it.

Some indication is given below of the kinds of auditory phenomena on which simple tasks can be carried out in a basic training programme. This will give an idea of how elementary the early exercises need to be. (What is often thought of as providing a simple listening task is work with minimal pairs, consisting of words differing only by one or another vowel sound occurring in an actual language. But in reality this is far too sophisticated to be presented to the ear and so to the attention of a person who has never practised listening to *anything*, and who besides has no previous acquaintance with distinctions operating within the overall vowel system of the language in question.) Much later, the various separate parameters can be superimposed in more complex combinations, graded up to resemble genuine language material more closely, and perhaps in the end moving towards the foreign language that is the object of study.

Summing up the threefold aim of basic auditory training: it is (1) to give practice at directing the attention and making decisions on what one has heard; (2) to de-condition each listener from exclusive dependence on the mother tongue as the basis for all his auditory judgments; (3) to give to each learner some awareness of the possibilities of spoken language generally, and put him in a better state of readiness for whatever he may encounter in the language (or languages) he is to learn. Time given to these activities, so far from being wasted, is very definitely *time saved*, thanks to the more efficient use that will then be made of the many hours that must in any case be spent on a language.

All material has to be carefully graded, and to start with cannot be too simple whatever the age-group or standard of the learner. Though the manner of presentation will obviously be different with ten-year-olds from that suitable with grown-ups, all should be put through similar exercises at the start; material for adults can then be more steeply graded as found appropriate. With practice, concentration develops, decisions are taken more confidently and rapidly, powers of discrimination grow more refined, judgments become more reliable. Each type of exercise needs first to be explained, then demonstrated, then given a brief trial practice, before being presented systematically and at length. The utterances themselves can be given live or in recorded form; a recording, even if of good quality, will prove more taxing since listeners have not the advantage of *seeing* such things as the lip movements of a speaker. On the other hand, a recording obliges the listener to rely on his ear alone.

Auditory training exercises

A great variety of exercises can be done on sequences of CV (consonant + vowel) syllables, such as ba ba ba or ba be bi or ba da ga or ba de gi.

1 The number of syllables can be counted. (Notice that no doubtful or borderline cases such as often occur in languages need arise here.) Responses can be given orally in chorus or individually, or written down as a numeral or by ringing a number on a prepared sheet containing lists of numerals, or by holding up a cube, having a numeral on each of its six sides, so that the appropriate number (up to 6) is made to face towards the teacher.[1]

2 Odd-Man-Out. Either a vowel or a consonant can be varied (later,

[1] If each face of the cube is given a different, clearly distinguishable colour, each colour regularly associated with a given number (such as *blue* always for *two*, and so forth), the teacher can easily check visually, at great speed, on the performance of quite a large group. Other advantages of this technique of eliciting responses are: the participation of *every* member of a group in the decision-making is assured; much more ground can be covered than while questioning people separately; the teacher gets constant feed-back from the group as a whole, instead of being influenced by the promptest or loudest vocal responses, and he can for instance readily adjust the standard of a given task up or down;

one of each), thus ba ba bi ba or ba da li sa (for vowels), where the number 3 would be the correct response (the 'odd man out') in each case; or ba ba da ba or ba be di bu (for consonants), where the number 3 would again be correct.

3 Present/Absent. Deciding whether a designated vowel or consonant (i.e. one just sounded by the teacher) occurs at all in the sequence(s) to follow. Members of a group can be asked to raise a hand for Yes; a tick (for Yes) and a cross (for No) can be written down in the place for each answer; the response cube can have a tick and a cross incorporated on it, preferably on opposite sides – the tick can then do duty also for number 5 and the cross for 6, with various simple mnemonic devices for remembering which is which in the early stages.

4 Deciding whether the vowel to be heard *last* in a sequence of syllables has occurred previously in the utterance or not.

5 Deciding whether a designated syllable (e.g. da) or vowel (e.g. a) or consonant (e.g. d) occurs *more than once* in a sequence or not.

6 Deciding at what point in an utterance a designated syllable or vowel or consonant occurs, for instance whether before or after some other designated part of the utterance.

7 Deciding whether a syllable or vowel or consonant, to be identified by pronouncing it separately *after* a complete utterance, has occurred in the course of that utterance or not; or has occurred more than once in the utterance.

8 Same/Different. Deciding whether two juxtaposed utterances sound the same or not (tick or cross) with respect to, for example, only their vowels or only their consonants or both vowels and consonants. This type of exercise lends itself to grading up in difficulty, almost indefinitely: by increasing the number of syllables; or by articulating the sequence of sounds more rapidly; or by making vowels, or consonants, less obviously different from one another so that greater auditory discrimination has to be exercised; or by various combinations of the foregoing.

9 Longer/Shorter. A. Deciding which of two vowels (later, two continuant consonants occurring medially) in two separate utterances is the longer. To start with, the difference in length is made very obvious. B. Deciding in which syllable (later in which syllables) of a sequence a longer vowel (or consonant) occurs. C. Deciding, in advanced work,

---

he can watch over particular individuals, perhaps delaying for a second or two to accommodate the slower worker; and he can at any moment break off to work with one person at a time.

which of a larger number of different lengths occurs, e.g. very short, short, long, very long.

10 Deciding whether vowels have (or not) the feature of nasality; have (or not) a changing quality, i.e. diphthongisation; or have one or other or both of these characteristics. (This can later be combined with 9 above.)

11 Pitch. A. Deciding whether the pitch is steady or moving, in a succession of separate utterances. B. Deciding whether a moving pitch is rising or falling, with later elaborations on this theme. C. Deciding as between a number of pitch distinctions, in sequences of syllables of increasing span. (At some point, moving pitches interspersed with steady pitches should be imposed on changing vowel qualities, see 10 above.)

12 ABX. Two utterances are presented and then a third, and the task is to decide which of the first two the third matches (if it has been stated that it does match one or the other), or whether or not it matches the first or the second (if it has been stated that it may possibly not match either).

13 A fundamentally different procedure – and much more taxing – is to present an utterance and *then* ask some simple questions to which the response will be Yes or No, such as: Are there 4 syllables? Are the vowels the same or not? Are there any long vowels? Obviously, quite separate from the ability to recognise and rapidly analyse the characteristics of an utterance, something else is being trained here, namely the ability to retain an utterance accurately in the memory for an appreciable time, after hearing it only once or perhaps twice; but the capacity to do just this has considerable importance for all language work and is therefore well worth cultivating.

14 Vowel quality differences. In more advanced work, if it is not found unsuitable to introduce technical terms such as are used in phonetic descriptions, the task can be to recognise distinctions such as close/open, front/back, centralisation, lip-rounding, and so forth.

15 Similarly, the feature of voicing can be identified as being present or absent in consonants, or aspiration in voiceless plosives, or palatalisation, or clear/dark l, or open/closed syllables, and so forth.

16 At any point, in all sorts of exercises, a selection of exotic vowels and/or consonants can be introduced. These may well (but need not necessarily) include those to be encountered in the language of study. The more elaborate made-up sequences then resemble the meaningless words of traditional type (also known as nonsense words or logatoms) used for advanced ear-training in courses in phonetics. However, many of the above types of exercise (Present/Absent, Same/Different and so on) can be given, if so desired, using some exotic sounds but without having recourse to phonetic symbols as such.

17 Even where for clarity letter symbols are introduced to represent various sounds, the sounds themselves can be very effectively drilled by arbitrarily numbering off the symbols where they stand on the blackboard, then eliciting responses by number, whether orally, or jotting them down for calling out afterwards, or by means of the response cube.

2.4 Performance training

A person studying a language not his own will almost certainly want to be able to perform in it, that is to speak and pronounce it. Now it is well known that, even when in possession of all the facts about the pronunciation (that such and such sounds occur, under what circumstances and in what positions in words, and so forth), the learner of a foreign language may still be unable to pronounce it adequately himself. The reasons for this are clear: partly that some of the sounds and sound combinations are previously unknown to him, so since he has never articulated them before he may find difficulty in doing so; and partly because, thanks to his mother-tongue habits, he has got into the way of performing certain movements in a certain manner and so has difficulty in performing somewhat different movements when that is what is asked of him.

Self-observation

A most important point, too often overlooked, is that every normal speaker, while he in fact hears his own speech as he produces it, is not very good at noticing how he speaks, for reasons already given. Yet it is only by learning to 'monitor' his own performance *more efficiently* that he can adequately observe himself speaking. This is manifestly what is required, however, before he can possibly check for himself the correctness or otherwise of his performance on foreign language material and so make any necessary alterations. Self-observation is thus a prerequisite for successful execution, and the programme of ear-training outlined above is designed to improve this. It has to be admitted, though, that it is far less easy to notice what one has said oneself than to notice what someone else says;[1] hence the need to work at this. Here the teacher can help, as explained below.

[1] In this sense, listening to one's disembodied voice from a recording of it might be thought to facilitate matters. However, there are several counter-indications for such a procedure: first, to hear captured in recorded form one's faltering attempts at sequences of foreign articulations can be very discouraging – and even to hear the sound of one's own voice quality is found disconcerting by many; secondly, a recording may well prove misleading, even if its quality and the standard of reproduction are good, and it would

We will assume that the teacher has first noticed a pupil's way of pronouncing something, and has shown that he has noticed. Let us assume further that he has given the pupil any facts he thinks will help him to pronounce differently – if this is what is required – and moreover that the pupil has then been coached to the point where he can produce some new effect to the satisfaction of his teacher. This may well not be under control as yet, and will assuredly not yet have become a habit: for the new set of movements to become habitual it is next essential that the pupil should rehearse, i.e. pronounce many times, the proper actions. Inevitably this will be done largely when the teacher is not present, at times when the learner has only his own judgment to rely on. Clearly it is vital that he should monitor his own attempts accurately and reliably if time spent on rehearsal is to be put to good use. The teacher can now prepare the pupil, and check on his state of readiness, for private practice by getting him to *pronounce and then comment on his own performance*. Only when the comments – as to whether the sound or feature under scrutiny was well performed or not, at each attempt – coincide with the teacher's assessment of the same attempts can the teacher feel fairly confident that private practice on the point will be profitable. In other words, the pupil has to be brought to the stage where, when monitoring himself, he knows for a fact either that what he has just uttered *is* good enough to pass or that it is *not* good enough – and of course knows what to do about it to make it better. When this stage has been reached he can reasonably be left to his own devices, though further checking by the teacher will still be useful.

Psychological preparation

It is important that the learner should approach all oral execution in the right frame of mind: the activity should be seen as *a performance*, having analogies with other kinds of performance – such as ballroom dancing or playing the violin (disregarding here the *purpose* behind any performance). Now quite apart from the specific skills needed for each of these, with their precisely co-ordinated movements of various parts of the body and so forth, we have to consider the psychological effect on the individual of being involved in any sort of performance that is carried out not in private but *witnessed by others*.

---

certainly be unfair to make out that that is what a person 'really' sounds like; thirdly, it is by no means clear just from a recording what the speaker ought now to *do* to sound better; and finally, to study a recording unaided is an advanced exercise, completely beyond the average learner.

Probably no individual goes through life without finding himself in a number of situations that constitute for him some sort of ordeal: the student at an oral examination, the candidate being interviewed for a post, the teacher facing his first class – these are some of the occasions that one recalls. All will experience nervous and muscular tension at such moments; some manage to keep things sufficiently well under control, others feel overawed and find themselves to a greater or lesser extent incapacitated. Familiar symptoms are a quickening of the pulse, a dry mouth, breathlessness; in particular adolescents find themselves blushing or trembling, or they may tend to stammer when they speak; younger children are more likely to be completely tongue-tied or to melt into tears. Having to speak or act before unaccustomed numbers is intimidating at first and may remain so for a long time, so that, for some, even getting up in class to recite what has been learnt, or being called upon to read aloud out of a book, is itself an ordeal, to be dreaded in anticipation.

The point of making such observations here is to draw attention to the situation created by the mere fact that in foreign language work the oral performance is in a strange idiom, in attempting to use which every learner inevitably feels particularly awkward and inadequate, causing him to experience heightened nervousness and embarrassment, which then have undesirable repercussions on his performance. As young people grow up, all gain in self-confidence through a broadening of experience generally. People tend to grow out of shyness and self-consciousness just by being exposed to the situations that produce these feelings – hence the value of the rehearsal, the mock interview, the trial run and the like. But uttering the words and sentences of a foreign language is a special case: the speaker feels that he is not fully himself, that he is being asked to abandon some essential part of himself – hence the subconscious resistance and unwillingness to articulate the foreign sounds really well. If he were to attempt to put this feeling into words, he would probably say he 'feels such a fool'. It is essential to try to overcome this very natural reaction.

An approach that often helps is the device of conscious make-believe. Many people are able to keep at bay the sensation of doing violence to some inner person simply by speaking and behaving as if they were some *other* person! Most English-speaking people can make some attempt at an accent of English not their own: the British can usually put on something of an 'American' accent, the Southern Englishman can probably sound more like a 'Cockney' Londoner if he wants to, or can by his manner of speaking suggest an Irishman, a Yorkshireman or a Scot. Now, disregarding any inaccuracies and inconsistencies there may be in such an act, it should be noticed that many exotic sounds (articulations alien to the individual's normal speech) are produced with skill and confidence and *without embarrassment*. In a similar way, many a Frenchman can put on what is recognisably an English accent in his French, and conversely many a young English person can be heard mimicking with considerable accuracy a typical French way of speaking English. As he does so he is in fact substituting all kinds of French articulations and characteristic speech behaviour for their English equivalents, yet the striking thing is that many of these are never heard to cross his lips during the French lesson! The reason for all this is clear: a speaker can bring himself to make the strange noises and allow his speech apparatus to perform the unaccustomed actions *provided he can feel that he is acting a part*, that he is someone else, not representing himself. As long as he is saying words and sentences of the mother tongue he can still feel right with himself, no matter how outlandish the various effects he produces.

Advantage can be taken of this in the classroom situation: let the English learner of French imagine he *is* a French person – and similarly for other cases. If written material is already arranged in the form of a scene or playlet, or even in a straightforward dialogue consisting of question and answer, the set-up for make-believe of course comes ready-made. But even separate sentences or isolated everyday phrases have similar dramatic potentialities if handled in this way, namely rendered not in one's own person. The teacher can transform the whole situation if, instead of appearing to read from the book, he will glance up as he pronounces a sentence and look – not towards the class but aside as if addressing an imaginary interlocutor. Members of the class can then proceed to do likewise.

The teacher should not overact: an exaggerated delivery, whether of facial expression, or gesturing, or of the rise and fall of the voice, can become counter-productive, being seen as too absurd for real life and therefore itself shy-making. Let the teacher do no more than he would wish his pupils ideally to do in their turn: if he is training them – as he should be – to notice things they hear, there should be little need for exaggeration.

The above procedure is to be looked upon as in no sense comparable with the proper dramatic presentation of a play in a foreign language. In the nature of things it is only the best pupils who are likely to get selected for the roles, and only the less reserved and bashful who tend to come forward in the first place; whereas what is here described is recommended for its therapeutic value for all.

A stage that will have preceded the above, though it may be reverted to at any moment, is that of directing the attention of an individual to a specific point in his way of pronouncing something, together with any necessary description or demonstration prior to the actual detailed coaching. Psychologically, the important thing here is that the matter should be *faced*, and patiently *insisted upon*,[1] in a relaxed, friendly, but above all matter-of-fact and business-like way, showing clearly that 'this is a job we have to do' – then any embarrassment at the intimacy of the situation is avoided on both sides. In a similar kind of way, much of the unease one might normally feel at having parts of one's person inspected by others is inhibited before a doctor or dentist by the matter-of-fact attitude of the physician and the professional atmosphere of the occasion.

There is much to be said for rehearsing certain things *in chorus*: every member gets plenty of practice this way; and confidence is engendered in the more timid by being able to perform inconspicuously, as one of a group. Admittedly the teacher is at something of a disadvantage in that *individual* achievement is hard to monitor; but some alternation of choral and individual work can be very effective. Among the things that lend themselves to group performance are: the silent miming of jaw and lip movements as such; the alternation of vowels, such as easy and difficult, long and short, rounded and spread; the alternation of a voiced and voiceless fricative in a single long breath; basic intonation patterns. Obviously the teacher must first demonstrate exactly what is to be done, then at a given moment the class joins in. If all is going well, the teacher can drop out and pay more attention to individuals while the chorus continues.

One of the most prevalent defects of execution is using too little voice: many pupils when asked to say a word or sentence make so small a sound as to be practically inaudible, even at close range. Now speaking very quietly means using very little breath force and this has several disadvantages for performing aloud in a foreign language. For a start, at such low volume it is extremely difficult for a teacher to detect whether an utterance or particular parts of it are being correctly articulated or not. So the pupil can be exhorted to 'speak up' simply to assist the teacher. Besides this, when the amount of air being passed through the glottis is small, it becomes impossible for a speaker to keep his vocal cords in firm and steady vibration through 'voiced' sounds – as many languages require; or again, strong breath force contrasts with weak breath force in e.g. word-final position in many languages and it is essential to make clear when it is the strong breath force that is intended. In addition, the effect of

[1] Every teacher should be able to recognise at once when he has begun to put too much pressure on an individual: he should consciously and visibly relax, becoming less insistent, or simply move on.

many consonant articulations is made more definite, by firmer contact combined with stronger air pressure from behind; then the teacher can better judge whether they are correctly formed or not.

Now this low level of voice production, arising from too little force of expulsion of the breath, is often just a form of laziness, to be cured by pointing this out. But often it is a psychological problem: the speaker (or would-be speaker) is literally incapacitated by the effect upon him of the whole situation – the foreign language, the thought of potential criticism from the teacher, the presence of others, everything combines to paralyse the muscles so that even normal breathing is impeded. Something needs to be done to alleviate this condition, which can cause mental distress quite apart from the loss of voice. Breaking off, telling the pupil to take some deep breaths, to talk about something else, to walk about – anything to reduce the tension that has built up for this one person; no doubt some of the same techniques might be used by the actor afflicted with stage-fright. But ultimately the situation has got to be faced, with the sympathetic understanding and co-operation of the teacher.

As already mentioned, choral speaking submerges the individual in the group. Forgetting about the foreign language for a moment, let the class chant in their own language the days of the week or a few numbers, loudly, then much more loudly, then as loudly as possible. Get individuals to do the same alone. Then say to the 'patient': Supposing you heard a knock on the door, how would you say 'Come in'? ('Come in!') Now suppose you weren't heard, how would you say it? ('Come in!' more loudly.) Now imagine there's a carpet-cleaner (a lawn-mower) at work just outside, so the person still can't hear! This should produce the desired result, with perhaps some amusement also, anyhow some reduction of tension all round, including in the case of the afflicted member of the group.

Another approach to the psychological problem of 'small voice' is to take the group to some convenient hall or very large room, with one individual going up on the platform while the teacher and all the others are at the far end of the room. Ask the individual to recite the days of the week, then say: 'We can't hear you!' – even if untrue! By such means one or all can be brought to a realisation of what each is *capable* of doing, and this can have a reassuring and liberating effect and enable a rapid improvement to take place thereafter.

If a person tends to speak through clenched teeth, say: 'As a matter of interest, could you show me how wide you can open your mouth?' To one who seems to have difficulty in rounding and protruding the lips, say: 'Let me see, how would you whistle?' If the answer comes: 'I can't whistle', say: 'Well, how would you put your mouth if you were going to *try* to whistle?' To a person who really seems to make little movement of any kind while speaking, it may prove effective to make some light-hearted reference to a ventriloquist.

In conclusion: let every teacher be prepared to manipulate his own voice with some freedom, in demonstration; let him speak or intone crescendo until he is sounding abnormally loud; let him speak extremely fast, then extremely slowly; let him speak for a second or two on a mono-tone or, if the teacher is a man, let him go momentarily into his falsetto register. He should be capable of demonstrating intonation patterns without words, humming the pattern itself on m or la. He may feel ridiculous at times, but even supposing on occasion he makes himself actually so, any hilarity caused will only help to create a relaxed atmo-sphere – though things must not, with a youthful audience, be allowed to get too out of hand! But if the teacher has shown that he is capable of 'loosening up', his pupils should find it easier to do so.

Teaching techniques and procedures

A good proportion of the class time that is spent on pronunciation is devoted most usefully to identifying difficulties and dealing with one difficulty at a time. Then all the members of a group can be given some practice by taking each in rapid alternation and getting him to articulate one or more times a given sound or syllable, a given word or phrase, then commenting briefly on his efforts, in particular letting him know when he has done something exactly right and perhaps at once asking him to see whether he can do the very same again. This lays the foundation of conscious control over his own articulatory movements, and makes a beginning with the important next stage of new habit forming.

It must be made clear that many of the techniques here described, though it takes a little time to read an account of them, are often in opera-tion for periods of *a few seconds* only – just long enough to achieve their aim. If any given procedure seems not to be getting results, it should not be persevered with but discarded in favour of some other approach. What works with one pupil may not work with another; above all no time must be wasted. The short explanation is to be preferred to a fuller one; technical terms, symbols, even diagrams can often be dispensed with if practical results are obtainable without them. (It is here assumed that the learning of phonetic theory, or of symbols as such, does not form part of the instruction. If it does, obviously, technical terms and the rest may suitably be brought into the practical work for their own sake.)

There comes a point when separate articulatory difficulties can be surmounted by an individual with success, even several times running, but there is then the problem of integrating the newly learnt movements into the general flow of speech, when a great variety of movements follow one another so rapidly that the speaker is liable, as it were, to be caught unawares, since he no longer has the time to give *conscious* attention to what he is doing. This is the moment when the teacher's main function is to give reminders, bringing to the speaker's notice any remaining instances of faulty pronunciation, in particular of the item that has most recently been the object of concentrated effort; but subsequently drawing his attention to miscellaneous matters, any or all of which may have been tackled more systematically on earlier occasions. This is a procedure that can usefully follow the periods of private practice referred to above.

Ultimately, for integrating all the various acquired movements into fluent sequences, almost any phrase of a foreign language can be taken and meticulously rehearsed, thus bringing nearer the time when everything can be executed accurately without conscious thought. But conscious attention there must first be: sequences of half a dozen or more syllables should be practised aloud in private as slowly as is found necessary in order to get everything right and observe that it *is* right. Fluency is not to be equated with mere rapidity of syllable rate: the result of speaking faster while making specific errors can only be to commit a larger number of those errors in a given span of time – often with serious results for general intelligibility. Very few types of faulty articulation actually get put right by more rapid speaking; moreover, speed itself induces other errors.

Besides the auditory awareness which is always of primary importance, visual observation is also to be cultivated. The teacher should be able to demonstrate degrees of jaw opening and especially of lip-rounding, and correct any lack of, or excess of, movement by appeal to the visual sense of the pupil, who will almost certainly fail to realise what his mouth is doing until he has *seen* it (in a mirror). Only when he has got it to look right[1] will he be convinced that his own tactile and kinaesthetic sensations were previously inadequate or misleading. From then onwards – with frequent reminders – he can make steady progress.

On the other hand, tactile awareness can itself be cultivated; this is specially relevant for many 'difficult' consonants, where some part of the tongue has to touch or nearly touch a part opposite to it, and if this cannot well be seen. All the teacher can do is to describe what should be going on and then exhort the pupil to *feel* this; it will be a valuable supplement to what he can *see*.

[1] Individual physiognomy varies so much that the teacher will have to judge to what extent a pupil's mouth posture should or should not be made to look exactly like his own.

27

But in the end hearing is more important than either seeing or feeling. It is essential that while telling a pupil what he should do with his tongue or lips or showing him what the mouth articulation should look like, the teacher should draw his attention to the resultant sound.

Any demonstration by the teacher of how to say anything gains greatly in effectiveness by being at once *repeated by him identically*. This brings home the fact that the utterance is not being offered as a piece of real-life behaviour but that attention is to be directed to the manner of execution for its own sake; the fact of repetition is equivalent to saying in effect: Like this, do you see?

It is also very effective always if the teacher can demonstrate a right and a wrong pronunciation, especially what the pupil himself has just done or is inclined to do. Although the teacher's imitation should be as accurate as possible, a very slight exaggeration is permissible to bring a point home – though it is only fair that the pupil be told that it *is* an exaggeration.

Particularly with vowels – where tactile and visual cues (apart from lip movement) are few – the auditory effect is paramount. Even here, the learner's articulating mechanism can often be manipulated at a distance by devices such as telling him to *think of* such and such a sound, or to try to make his sound more like such and such, or to try to utter a sound which shall equally resemble two others. The teacher, provided he has adequate knowledge of his pupil's own language and of his manner of speaking it, may find it useful to start from something known in order to modify that in a certain way – but this must not be taken as an encouragement to be satisfied with rough approximations.

Finally, the timing and manner of intervention by the teacher in the pupil's delivery of foreign words and sounds may be crucial to a successful outcome. Pedagogical considerations include such factors as the need to preserve the flow of instruction when, in the judgment of the teacher, the matter in hand might be too greatly interfered with by distracting remarks about pronunciation – though he may find ways of giving unobtrusive reminders in passing. Psychological considerations – important for obtaining and retaining the co-operation of the pupil, on which every-thing depends – may on occasion prompt the teacher to overlook some imperfection, or wait for another opportunity, possibly out of class, for raising the matter if too much criticism in front of others might have been resented. However, in the learning situation all must be prepared to accept adverse comment, though in the case of pronunciation this is bound to be of a very personal nature, and may be subconsciously inter-preted as an assault on the personality; hence the need for judgment and tact of a high order.

2.5   Phonetic notation and its uses

Phonetic notation consists of a set or system of signs or written symbols, which tie in closely with events and sequences of events occurring when a language is spoken. Thus although they appear in written form these symbols relate, and are devised with the intention of relating, to things happening in the spoken medium of language. They can therefore be looked upon as a visual aid to the study of spoken language.

The usefulness of any particular notation, or set of symbols, can be assessed only in relation to the purpose it is intended to serve and to how well it achieves that purpose. There are some purposes to which no phonetic notation should be put – for instance, it is incorrect to think that the aim of phonetic notation is to teach or help a person to pronounce better the sounds of a foreign language! What a phonetic notation can do is to show what are the proper sequences of sound units for any given word or sentence of a language, and it does this very well – provided the values of the symbols are known and *once the sounds they stand for have been learnt*. But no phonetic symbol can teach the pronunciation of a sound: it can only indicate, and act as a visual reminder of, where in words each unit occurs – specially helpful when, as often happens, the conventional orthographic system (the ordinary spelling) of a language does not do so, or not consistently. Besides this, a phonetic notation can be made to show things that would not and in many cases should not be indicated in an orthography.

Forms of phonetic notation

It should now be clear that the *means used* for indicating the presence of a given sound unit in a sequence is a secondary consideration, of typographical nature only. There may be reasons of expediency, such as legibility or printer's costs, for adopting one letter shape or set of letter shapes in preference to others, but such factors are of minor significance in relation to the function of notation as such. Other things being equal, clarity and simplicity and even elegance are naturally worth striving for in themselves but linguistic and pedagogical considerations must come first: sometimes too great simplification can do violence to linguistic facts and pedagogical aims may be better achieved by some means that results in complicating the visual presentation. As there are bound to be divergent views on such matters, sets of phonetic symbols can differ in appearance even when meant to serve the same purpose; in addition to this, the purpose may itself differ somewhat. So in any case inconsistencies are inevitable as between one author or printer and another, one period and another, one language and another, even with one writer at different times. As a result, any complete standardisation of usage, convenient though it might be, is doubtless unobtainable.

The values attached to symbols, then, are not something immutable, but are in any case *conventional*. Now whatever written form language takes, conventions are bound to operate between it and speech; once established, these are implicit as opposed to being stated at every point in the text. Since conventions can be varied, it follows that different forms of notation can and do arise.

The question now to be discussed is what use, if any, can or should be made of phonetic notation – regardless of the details of its construction or appearance – by the teacher of pronunciation. We must leave out of account the fact that the ultimate decision whether or not to use notation may not be in the hands of the individual teacher but depend on educational policy, the views or preferences – even the prejudices – of higher authority. And we need not here consider the requirements of phoneticians, dialectologists or other specialists but only the practising language teacher, whether of groups or individuals.

A phonetic notation should not be taught for its own sake but as a means to an end. When the end can be achieved by other means as effectively and in a shorter time, there is no virtue in learning to handle phonetic symbols. For instance, numbers may conveniently be allotted to the vowels of a language and these can then be written down from dictation or called out by teacher or pupil without possibility of ambiguity or doubt. An orthographic text can be annotated, in part or throughout, with superscript numbers, either on the blackboard for identification of the sounds to be pronounced, or set as a task or test. At the point where this type of procedure ceased to be practical because of the clumsiness or illegibility of the result, the question would arise whether a set of phonetic symbols might not have been better introduced in the first place. But other factors such as the aim and length of the course would come in here; only the teacher is in a position to decide.

The location of strong stresses in a word or sentence can easily be shown on an orthographic text, in handwriting with one or more superscript accents or with underlining, in print or typescript by the use of capitals or italics.

Intonation requires its own marking. This can be as simple as will show the rise and fall of the voice in general outline, perhaps separate from the text, or interlined with it; or it can be a more sophisticated system of marks used in accordance with carefully worked out conventions. Again it is worth pointing out that the teacher must decide in the light of all the circumstances what result he wants to obtain and how best to obtain it in the time available. And again the point should be stressed that no great merit attaches to mastering a system of notation as such, but that it is only useful to the extent to which it achieves its object. Where intonation is concerned the important thing is that any visual signs used should link up with the actual sound that the marks stand for; the only way to ensure that they do is by copious ear-training practice.

2.6 Priorities

The work of the pronunciation teacher will be much facilitated if he establishes in his own mind some order of priorities. Obviously some things are more important than others, some things are bound to take up more time than others; some procedures are particularly relevant in view of features peculiar to the target language, some points give more trouble to learners of one nationality than those of another and will therefore need, or not need, to have special attention devoted to them. But while it will always be true to say that pronunciation has in the end to be acquired by individuals, each of whom is different, a fair amount of generalisation can reasonably be attempted when it comes to setting out, as is done in Parts 3 and 4 below, the phonetic features of one language that are most likely to be found troublesome to acquire by the speakers of another.

There follows a suggested set of Categories, of general application, that provide a framework within which to classify the interference and other phenomena that one encounters in foreign language learning. N.B. The Categories should not be looked upon as establishing the priorities for a teacher: he should work out the priorities in relation to his own course of instruction and to the people following it. Thus at a given point in time some item in, say, Category *B* or *C* may take priority over some item belonging to Category *A*. It will usually be found that characteristic difficulties group themselves into quite a small number of items, falling into one or other of the Categories set up below; these are made the basis for the Inventories at the end of Parts 3 (p. 53) and 4 (p. 88).

Category *A* is for distinctions between *one phoneme of a language and another phoneme of the same language*, giving rise to actual or potential minimal pairs of words differing in meaning in the language concerned by the substitution of the one for the other. No pronunciation of a foreign language can be considered adequate that does not satisfactorily distinguish between all its separate phonemes.

Category *B* is for anything in a person's way of speaking a foreign language which, though not causing one word to be pronounced in place of another, is *judged to constitute a gross or marked foreign accent.*

Category *C* is for mispronunciations that are not particularly serious in themselves but might well receive attention because they are *comparatively easy to put right without much expenditure of time.* In many cases all that is needed is that the learner should have his attention directed to the point and should be put in possession of relevant facts.

Category *D*. This covers matters that may be quite difficult for the foreign learner to get right, even with the expenditure of some time and trouble, but which *contribute notably to authenticity of pronunciation* and may well on occasion call forth favourable comment from natives on the 'good accent' of the speaker. Items in this Category deserve attention principally with students who are aiming at a really high overall standard. However, there could well be differences of opinion as to whether an item should be placed in this Category rather than in Category *B*.

Category *E*. Miscellaneous items of a phonetic nature that might be held to constitute *finer points* in the pronunciation of a language. University students, teachers in training, and those taking specialised courses in phonetics or linguistics would all benefit from the theory and practice of the various matters involved. Even within this Category it would no doubt be possible to identify features as being of greater or lesser importance, but to extend the Categories formally beyond the five here set up would prove of limited utility.

3 Teaching speakers of English to pronounce other languages

3.1 Facial movement

English is a language that can be spoken with relatively little movement of the jaw and lips. Indeed, in ordinary talking, many mother-tongue speakers of English appear to move their mouths hardly at all. This absence of visible facial activity may remind one of the performance of a ventriloquist.

Those whose profession often requires that their words should reach large audiences without benefit of microphone, such as stage actors and politicians, have to move their mouths about far more vigorously if they are to make a success of their speaking in public and be known as 'good speakers' (and also have to learn to make *louder* sounds than in more normal everyday situations). Some do this instinctively from the start, others learn only gradually. But even actors and politicians indulge in very much less facial activity (besides producing a smaller volume of sound) when speaking ordinarily and talking to not more than one or two.

Now what has just been said is fairly obvious and will be familiar to most people, yet many do not realise the extent of their own ineffectiveness as speakers or know what to do to improve. Teachers and lecturers far and wide exert themselves too little when addressing their hearers though all are *capable* of speaking more audibly and distinctly: observe how, to secure the initial attention of an audience, a person will give out some introductory announcement loud and clear – whether it be 'Ladies and gentlemen!' or 'May I have your attention, please?' or even 'Well, boys and girls, . . .' or 'Right, let's begin!'

The above applies of course to those of any nationality, not specially to the English. But English-speaking people need to realise that *for any given size of audience and at any given level of sound* most other languages are spoken with markedly greater activity and visible movement of the lips and jaw. This fact needs pointing out to every English learner of a foreign language, as a useful generalisation which can then be qualified according to the characteristics of the language of study. But it is not enough for the fact to be baldly stated and left at that: it must be brought home to the English learner that a new kind of speech behaviour is being asked of him and that this can only be acquired through assiduous, systematic and quite specific practice. Analogies with other physical activities can be suggested at this point, which may help to lessen some of the real unease that people tend to feel when told in effect that they are to pull strange faces – especially in front of others. (This embarrassment, quite understandably, can also afflict a teacher at times.) So let the pupil first call to mind an action such as that of opening and closing a hand, or opening and shutting the eyes, and then proceed to rehearse the raising and lowering of the jaw, the opening and shutting of the mouth, the vigorous alternate rounding and spreading of the lips.

A two-fold purpose is served by doing some facial gymnastics: exercising the various muscles will be 'limbering up' for performing movements and combinations of movement that have to be executed in pronouncing the foreign language – particularly since the native English-speaker commonly makes rather *little* movement as he speaks; and doing the exercises brings familiarity with previously unknown and unaccustomed sensations and so dispels some of that self-consciousness which is experienced by most people learning a foreign language.

Once it is accepted that facial movement should be deliberately rehearsed and not just referred to in passing – if at all – there is much to be said for carrying out exercises in some systematic fashion. Flexing the jaw up and down is a good first step. The jaw should be dropped to the fullest extent, then returned to the position of teeth clenched (taking care not to bite the tongue in the process!); with voice, this will resemble a - i - a - i. The performer should watch the lower part of his own face in a hand mirror (not necessarily in class), and a vivid impression of the movement is gained if this is carried out in complete silence. The exercise should be done first very slowly, concentrating on maximum extent of each movement; then faster. Just as deep breathing exercises involve more expansive movement than normal breathing, so these jaw movements should be deliberately made as wide as possible, far wider than would ever be required during speaking. A later variation is to make smaller up and down movements as fast as possible for several seconds.

An entirely different exercise, in a sense complementary to the above but for the purpose of cultivating awareness of motion of the tongue in the mouth, is to *fix* the jaw position by for instance making the upper and lower front teeth touch at their edges, and *while keeping them in contact* articulate a - i - a - i with sudden transitions between the two vowels. In normal speaking of course, in almost any language the alternation a - i - a - i or equivalent will be carried out with simultaneous jaw *and*

34

tongue movement; but the exercise is valuable for drawing attention to the fact that vowel quality is dependent on resonances created by (among other things) the particular configuration of the parts of the mouth and pharynx *not* occupied by the tongue. Realisation of this is particularly helpful when working at front rounded vowel articulations, see p. 36 below.

Lip-rounding

Lip-rounding means forming a small hole at the lips; this is a position of the mouth that is required for certain vowels. (There cannot be many languages having *no* (lip-)rounded vowels, but on the other hand the total of rounded vowels occurring never outnumbers those without rounding.) Just bringing the two lips close to each other vertically does not constitute 'rounding' properly speaking, which requires that the two *corners* of the mouth be drawn closer together from each side. In this sense it is correct to say that English is normally spoken with very little rounding at all. What there is is not very marked, and statistically few of the English vowels have even that. Many other languages are spoken with a great deal more lip-rounding in the sense that it is much more marked, that a higher proportion of the separate vowels of these languages have lip-rounding (of this more vigorous kind), and that the frequency of occurrence of such vowels is greater in any continuous run of syllables in connected speaking. For instance, while a French person is speaking the lips are in a rounded position for quite one third of the time; while English is being spoken the lips have their much less vigorous rounding less than half as frequently. Now each time the lips are rounded they have subsequently to be spread, so in terms of the number of *movements* whether of rounding or spreading, the English person may note that in speaking French the number of quite vigorous changes of lip position for vowels is roughly equal to the number of words in an utterance. In Spanish and Italian the frequency of rounded vowels is not quite as high as in French, in German it is lower still though higher than in English; and in all three languages the rounding (as in French) is executed more vigorously than is usual in English.

The basic exercise for lip-rounding and spreading is simply to alternate i - u - i - u with maximum movement. This can be performed rhythmically by the group all together, whether with voice or in silence; for acquiring a further measure of control the movement can be carried out at irregular intervals but on a word of command, thus: Whistle!...grin!... whistle!...grin!

An additional point to be noted is that by a different use of the muscles round the oral aperture the lips can take up two rather different shapes, for *both* of which the corners are drawn together as described above. These can be termed 'pursing' and 'pouting' respectively. 'Pursing' means tucking the lips in towards the teeth so that less of each lip shows externally; 'pouting' means pushing the lips out away from the teeth as if one were 'pointing with one's mouth', forming a trumpet-shape with more of each lip showing externally. Though it is customary in speaking English neither to 'purse' nor to 'pout' much, it can be observed that when urged to round the lips more vigorously most English people tend to 'purse' rather than to 'pout'. For the type of strong rounding used in many languages they should 'pout' and not 'purse'.[1]

The difference between the two should be clearly demonstrated by the teacher, and then pupils should be encouraged to experiment in private before a mirror. A good way to draw attention to the trumpet-shape is to hold the mouth in this position *throughout* the articulation of an *English* sentence, regardless of the appropriateness or otherwise of lip-rounding for particular sounds. This is very effective for showing that the type of muscular tension that makes the mouth look like a trumpet can be held at various degrees of jaw lowering and with various sizes of actual opening at the lips. For the 'open lip-rounding' of French 'open *o*' as in *comme* kɔ̃m, German 'short *o*' as in *noch* nɔx, the *protrusion* of the lips is still quite marked, though the jaw is lower and the mouth opening larger as compared to the 'close lip-rounding' of French 'close *o*' as in *beau* bo, German 'long *o*' as in *wohl* vol.

Needless to say, countless reminders that the lips should *be* rounded, and of *how* they should be rounded, will continue to be required.

Front rounded vowels

Two parameters of tongue-advancing/retracting and lip-rounding/spreading operate in a regular association in English (and in many, indeed most, other languages), the relationship being that as the lips round, the body of the tongue retracts, and vice versa. In some languages, notably German and French, but also the languages of Scandinavia including Finnish, as well as Hungarian, Turkish and a number of others, the two parameters function independently of one another to the extent that the lips can also round while the tongue is *advanced* in the mouth. So for any given type of lip position there are two potential tongue positions, namely

[1] An unusual feature of Norwegian and of Swedish is that two otherwise rather similar vowels occur in the system, for one of which the lips have to be distinctly 'pursed' while for the other they have to be quite strongly 'pouted'. A separate parameter operates here which is not catered for in the traditional classification of lip positions for vowels.

36

more advanced and more retracted, and this can and does give rise to quite separate and different-sounding vowels of the language. Those vowels for which the tongue is advanced and the lips rounded are termed 'front rounded vowels', and because of the unfamiliar combination of positions of the organs their proper pronunciation causes immense difficulty to the speaker of a language, such as English, that does not have them. It is essential that the necessary independence of lips and tongue should be gained; to develop this demands inescapably some hard work.

Two main approaches are: to practise keeping the tongue steady and bunched at the front while moving the lips, and conversely to practise keeping the lips steady and strongly rounded while moving the tongue. The former gives an exercise that can be represented by i - y - i - y, the second gives u - y - u - y. (y is the phonetic symbol used to stand for 'French *u*', German *ü* (*u* modified), which are both typical front rounded vowels.) For once, while first acquiring control, the English learner will do well to disregard anything he *hears* and concentrate instead on the movements and muscular sensations. (Listening and recognition practice on these vowels is to be done separately, and may have preceded performance training.)

1 (i - y - i - y) To achieve y at the outset the pupil should start with the lips strongly spread, as in a broad grin, while sounding i and directing the attention to the sensation in the mouth of the tongue tip pressing forward against the lower front teeth, and the sides of the tongue pressing up against the gums of the molars. He should seek to intensify these sensations by consciously pressing harder, and by alternating this a few times with return to a position of rest.

The next step is to keep thinking of i (imagining one *is saying* i) and, while retaining awareness of the sensations in the mouth bring the lips round firmly to the whistle position (practised previously). The result should give i - y. It will help to think of whistling a very *high* note – indeed a person who is unable to whistle high is failing to get his tongue far enough forward to articulate y. If the rounding itself is correct but the resultant sound unsatisfactory, the instruction should be to try to whistle a higher note.

The above simple exercise should be carried out several times. The temptation will be to let the tongue slip back, either while the lips are being rounded or very soon after; the clue is to concentrate on retaining the i sensations inside the mouth. Continuous alternation of the positions for i and y should then be rehearsed on one breath.

When y is attempted following various consonants, lip-rounding *during the consonant* should be insisted upon. Otherwise French *vu* is liable to sound not very different from Eng. *view*, owing to the rounding being carried out too late. In most contexts the chief problem is to get the tongue forward, without which French *vu* is liable to sound little different from *vous*.

A further complication that may well arise is due to the fact that the so-called 'back' vowel of Eng. *food* is now pronounced with so much fronting of the tongue by so many English-speakers that their attempts at *vous* are quite likely to sound too much like *vu*! (This 'fronting' has long been known in some forms of Scottish speech, as shown by spellings such as *guid* for *good*.) A more back quality for the sound in French *vous*, and especially for that in German *Kuh*, can often be achieved just by careful imitation of the model; increasing the vigour of the lip-rounding is also quite likely to help. The suggestion of trying to whistle the *lowest* possible note can sometimes prove effective.

When more rapid speaking is attempted (by advanced students) the common tendency is to omit or skimp the lip-rounding for y; *vu* then sounds and looks practically like *vie*. Adequate work earlier on the rounding/spreading exercise described above ought to have done something to check this tendency; ultimately, reminders and the necessary insistence should prevail.

2 (u - y - u - y) Strong lip-rounding should be fixed at the start of this exercise and kept unaltered. The change of tongue position should be made in both directions as smartly as possible so as to intensify awareness of sensations inside the mouth; sudden alternation of high and low whistled notes obtains the same effect. Starting from u, the instruction should be to do one's best to pronounce i (while firmly holding the rounded posture for u unchanged). To get the proper auditory effect for y the smallness of the aperture at the lips is more crucial than extreme fronting of the tongue; 'thinking of i' may induce some opening at the lips, so then the instruction should be: Make the hole smaller! It should be pointed out, and insisted upon, that during sequences such as *voulu*, *tout vu*, the lips are rounded *throughout* and that the two vowel sounds should be produced with no visible difference in mouth posture.

3 With the tongue only very slightly less bunched up in the mouth another front rounded vowel is formed, for acquiring which precisely analogous techniques are to be put into operation. This is of the type found in French, as in *deux* dø, and German *ö* (long *o* modified) as in *böse* bøzə. In each language, this relates to a corresponding back vowel of the type of French 'close *o*' as in *dos* do, German 'long *o*' as in *wo* vo, as y relates to u; and to a corresponding front *non*-rounded vowel of the type of

French *né* ne, German *Tee* te, as y relates to i. The following diagram expresses the relationship:

```
i  y  u
e  ø  o
```

Particular points to note are that the two rounded vowels in the lower series (o ø) have lip-rounding almost as tight as the top series, and that for all three of the lower series the tongue is only very slightly lower than for those of the top. The differences in notation, and familiar associations with some of the letters of the roman alphabet, encourage the English person to imagine that the differences between the two sets of vowels are greater than is in fact the case. The various faults of pronunciation that speakers of English tend to have with the three vowels of the lower series can all be reduced and often cleared up entirely by getting it firmly fixed in the mind that in e - ø - o the differences from i - y - u are *extremely small.*

When attempting ø the English student invariably has an overpowering urge to pronounce ɜ, the normal English 'hesitation-vowel'[1] generally spelled out as 'er...',[2] and which also occurs (for 'R-droppers', see p. 58) in English words variously spelt as in *turn, girl, heard, work*, and exceptionally *colonel.* The characteristic English mispronunciation of this vowel is faulty in three respects: the lips are *not rounded*, the tongue is *not front enough*, and it is *not close enough.* The lip-rounding is best dealt with by working the progression from u to y and then dropping the jaw only a little, while retaining tight rounding, to ø. But attending to the lips alone is unlikely to produce a satisfactory result. For the close front tongue position required it is essential that the performer should first be able to articulate e, so that by aiming at e, and imagining he *is saying* e while maintaining tight rounding, the result is ø. The trouble is that a vowel as close as French or German e is not habitual to most speakers of English[3] (though of course all are familiar with still closer vowels of the i type). The instruction for all attempts at e that are not close enough should therefore be: More like i, more like i! The closer position once attained, this should then be kept and lip-rounding added – giving ø. If the lip-rounding is

---

[1] Not for Scots who hesitate on e.
[2] It is noteworthy that the French 'hesitation-vowel' is ø, strongly lip-rounded. Spanish and Italian, having no front rounded and no central vowel (ɜ is a central vowel), hesitate on ɑ. Speakers of many languages, when lost for a word, tend to close the mouth and so hesitate on m. English-speakers also often close the mouth *after* their hesitation-vowel and so articulate 'erm...' (ɜm).
[3] Though it is found in some regional varieties of English, e.g. among Scots, in Wales and in North-East England, as the vowel in *day.*

satisfactory but the sound is too open, say: More like y! If the tongue
tends to move back (centralise) when the lips round, say: Think of e!

4 A third and much more open front rounded vowel occurs in French
and in German: this is the sound in French *seul* sœl, German *zwölf*
tsvœlf, which enters into a third series of vowel qualities, related analo-
gously to the previous two as follows:

i y u
e ø o
ɛ œ ɔ

The English learner tends to pronounce œ with no lip-rounding at all,
merely substituting his English 'shwa' vowel ə (as in *another* ənʌðə.[1]) The
'pouting' lip posture is essential here,[2] but with the jaw well dropped. It is
worth pointing out that in spite of the similarities in spelling (French *eu*,
German *ö*, for both ø and œ), the jaw and lip position, the tongue position
and the auditory effect all make ø more different from œ than from y; the
same could be said in relation to the other vowels of the middle series.

In conclusion, lip-rounding in general is a *continuing* problem for
English-speakers: with growing fluency the tendency is for rounding,
even once learnt, to lapse. Continued vigilance and insistence must therefore be the order of the day for every foreign language teacher.

3.2 Management of the breath

Sequences of vocal sounds produced by speakers of all languages result
from modification and manipulation of the outgoing airstream as it comes
from the lungs and passes up and out through the throat and mouth.
(There are certain exceptions, none of which are relevant here.) Depending on the various ways in which modification of the airstream can take
place the sounds will be more, or less, prominent to the ear of a hearer; it
is often quite easy to hear which parts of a sequence stand out more than
others.

One of the ways of making the vocal sound more prominent, or less so,[3]

[1] He will also be tempted to *lengthen* his sound whenever œ comes under strong stress:
he is unable to identify œ fully with ə since ə itself is never strongly stressed, so instead
he makes something more like ɜ (which is long). It should be noticed that for German
this is invariably wrong since German œ is always short.
[2] It may be observed that the *French* 'shwa' vowel is articulated with this kind of
rounding also.
[3] Other ways of varying the prominence of sounds, syllables or words include:
manipulation of the rise and fall of the voice (see Pitch variation, p. 47), varying
length of a vowel or a consonant, slowing or speeding the rate of utterance, inserting
pauses, and all kinds of combinations of the foregoing.

is by exerting muscles down in the chest to press differently on the air in the lungs and so expel a varying amount of air with each push or pulse. More vigorous effort tends, as one might expect, to make the resultant sound louder – other things being equal – and vice versa. One can *hear* whether or not a sound is louder, one can *feel* whether or not more effort is being expended as one speaks; usually the two work in the same direction, though it is possible for them to be at variance, for a relatively greater effort *not* to be perceived as a relatively louder sound.

Strong stress

The type of manipulation of the airstream with which we are here concerned makes differences observable between successive *syllables*, one of which is more prominent than another only by virtue of the greater effort expended on it. The technical term for effort expended during speaking is 'stress'. Syllables having the greater effort are called 'strongly stressed' or simply 'stressed' relative to others which are termed 'weakly stressed' or 'unstressed'.

Languages differ markedly from one another in the use they make of differences of stress: some languages have big differences between amounts of stress, particular syllables having heavy stress and others very much less. These are known as stress languages, and stress differences are closely tied up with the structure of their words, each word of more than a single syllable having at least one syllable that bears strong stress. Speakers of such languages, of which English is one, naturally learn which syllable in a word this is and always give it a suitable amount of stress when they say the word. When they set about speaking other languages they naturally carry over their habit of stressing some syllables strongly and others less strongly. For speaking other stress languages (e.g. German) all the English person needs to know is *where* to put strong stresses in any sequence of syllables; he may very well make 'mistakes of stress' through not knowing this. But any dictionary of words of these languages is bound to mark in some way the syllables that bear strong stress, so it is a simple matter to find the facts. Then, in a sentence, most though not all of these syllables will in fact be strongly stressed together with numerous words of one syllable whose stress pattern obviously does not have to be separately indicated; and where all the stresses fall will be in conformity with the usages of the given language.

Now many languages do not make use of stress in this kind of way: first, it can be quite hard to decide which are the more prominent syllables, on hearing the language spoken; then, they may be prominent for reasons other than strong stress and therefore not stand out consistently but vary according to conditions at the time, such as their position in a group, or the intonation used. Speakers of such languages, called non-stress languages, often have little sense of stress and do not feel inside them some pulses to be markedly stronger than others. In their own usage they may vary apparently haphazardly, and they hardly seem to mind whether one syllable rather than another *is* made to stand out when they hear their language spoken by foreigners. It is as if they were actually rather insensitive to stress phenomena – and so indeed they have become, through long conditioning, since in their case stress would have been one of the features to which they would have learnt not to respond (p. 14). English-speakers on the contrary are so sensitive to stress phenomena, through their conditioning, that even children and others untrained notice at once when foreign speakers seem to misplace a stress, and can pinpoint the error and describe or correct it.

When English-speakers attempt a language of this fundamentally different type (e.g. French or Spanish) they have first to learn – and they find it far from easy – *not* to carry over their in-built habit of coming down heavily on some syllables and not on others. Which syllables they involuntarily emphasise in saying a given phrase will depend on various factors: it may be that the form of a word suggests an English word having a particular stress pattern, which they therefore reproduce; it may be that the appropriate rise and fall of the voice suggests strong stresses in some way combined or correlated with it; or it may be that the rhythmical succession of stresses to which they are accustomed (see p. 68) induces a strong stress for no other reason than that one was due to fall just then.

Syllable-timing

It is far easier to learn to alter the placing of strong stresses, to put a stress on a different syllable, than to resist the urge to place a strong stress somewhere or other on every important word. After the facts have been described and demonstrated by the teacher, the basic requirement for a satisfactory result in performance is practice at 'syllable-timing'. Syllable-timed languages (the converse of stress-timed languages, see p. 68) have their syllables uttered at quite a regular rate right through a group of words, until the speaker comes to the end of his sentence or takes a fresh breath in the course of it. Every syllable of the group sounds as if it carries a certain importance, none being much more or much less audible than the rest, and the general effect is of something steady and mechanical, like the ticking of a clock. Learners should be put through exercises, starting with regular tapping of one finger on a table twenty or more times as fast as possible; then the articulation of ba ba ba ba . . . similarly; then, after demonstration by the teacher, performing an *English* sentence with syllable-timing in order to become aware of how *wrong* it sounds and therefore how different syllable-timing is from the normal English stressing of words. Children learning French can have their attention drawn to the 'Daleks' (artificial beings familiar from television) whose mechanical nature is suggested by getting the actors to speak with syllable-timing – as well as with other unnatural features such as short gaps between syllables. It may also be noted that Indians, Pakistanis and especially West Indians tend to speak English with syllable-timing.

It needs to be pointed out here that syllable-timing is not absolute but only a tendency, and that languages which have it may also have other features that disturb its strict operation. For instance, the lengthening of vowel sounds at certain points in French or Italian, the frequent doubling of consonant sounds in Italian, introduce minor variations in a strict rhythm. Moreover in these languages one can perfectly well convey special emphasis by leaning quite heavily on certain syllables as required, without however interfering much with the steady rhythmic syllable flow. But the English learner should aim at basic regularity during his practising, and may note that French will not be felt strange or wrong even when whole strings of syllables are uttered with *absolute* regularity of timing, odd though this may sound to English ears. This is very striking coming from French *children* as they speak or read aloud; they have not yet learnt to manipulate the expressive and other deviations from strict syllable-timing that get mastered by the more mature speaker.

Centralisation

It is possible for stress-timed and syllable-timed languages to have developed from a common stock. Whenever stress-timing is in operation, or comes into operation, a complementary tendency is also at work: the tendency to reduce the force on syllables that do *not* receive a strong stress. This has the effect of weakening them so that ultimately in particular cases whole syllables, vowels as well as consonants, just drop out and in a later stage of the language no longer get pronounced.

An intermediate stage before a vowel disappears altogether ('elision', see Glossary) is when it is sounded very lightly and at the same time the tongue does not move as far as it used to in forming the articulation. Taking into account the various places towards which the tongue could be moving and the position it would have occupied just previously, it can

43

usually be shown that the tongue in each case literally does not go so far out of its way; the result is 'centralisation'. The general principle of economy of effort is seen at work in the lesser tongue movements correlated naturally with the reduction in breath force.

Languages that possess a weak central vowel, as English does, have incorporated the above tendency into their sound system. Other languages that have no central vowel in their system (e.g. Spanish, Italian, Greek) either have virtually no centralisation or do have a perceptible amount in certain cases.

English-speaking people have to resist their natural tendency to centralise the tongue when reducing breath force on syllables. They should disregard entirely the slight centralisation of vowels sometimes found in other languages, referred to above, since they will always be in danger of centralising too much and in the wrong places: as English has a fully central unstressed vowel in its system, the English-speaker is tempted to produce this whenever the conditions promote it. The two most frequent and most noticeable cases are: (1) centralisation of fully open ɑ-vowels to a quality resembling ə; and (2) centralisation of close front i-vowels to a quality like English 'short I' as in *bit*. Examples follow:

(1) the first syllable of It. *salata*, *patate*, Ger. *Maschine*, *Kaninchen*, Fr. *madame*, *Marie*; the middle syllable of Fr. *journaliste*, *Italie*; the last syllable of It. *signora*, Sp. *señora*; very prevalent in the French feminine definite article *la*, which in fluent speaking is liable to sound indistinguishable from English attempts at *le*, so may give the impression of incorrect use of gender forms. This type of mistake is best dealt with by concentrating on a wide mouth opening while dropping the jaw, so leading to a fully open posture of the tongue.

(2) the first syllable of Fr. *immense*, *système*; the middle syllable of Fr. *ordinaire*, *politesse*, *quantité*, It. *storico*, *trinità*. This mistake, and the tendency to centralise in general, is best dealt with by helping the pupil to form a clear mental picture of each foreign vowel as an entity, with its characteristic quality together with any other of its attributes; by making sure that he learns in which words a given vowel occurs; and by insisting that he aims at the vowel quality concerned while remaining on guard against any, more central, variation from it.

3.3 Activity at the larynx

The complex physiological movements within the larynx resolve basically, for the purposes of the foreign language learner, into the vibration and the non-vibration of the vocal cords known as voicing or 'voice' and 'breath' respectively. The complication for inter-linguistic purposes is in the *timing* of the two activities relative to other things going on at the same moment, and here there are marked differences between languages. Wherever such differences in speech behaviour exist, there will be found problems for the learner of a foreign language.

Aspiration

This term is given to the delayed onset of vibration of the vocal cords following the release of a voiceless plosive (p t k). The majority of speakers of English 'aspirate' whenever the following vowel is strongly stressed, except when s precedes the plosive; so they aspirate in *park*, *take*, *Kate* but not in *spark*, *stake*, *skate*. A study of the diagram below will make clear what is involved. A horizontal line represents a sequence of events on a time track moving from left to right. The line is straight ——— when the vocal cords are not in vibration, wavy ∿∿∿∿ when they are. The vertical line marks the point in time when the plosive (p t or k) is released.

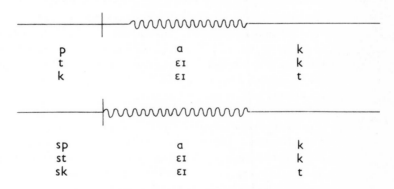

In weakly stressed syllables aspiration is very slight or negligible. Some English-speakers regionally (e.g. Yorkshire) or idiosyncratically do not aspirate.

For learning German the English-speaker does not have to give a thought to aspiration since English speech habits are similar. (Actually, many South Germans, including Swiss and Austrians, do not aspirate.)

For all Romance and all Slav languages aspiration is inappropriate and should be corrected if at all noticeable. The extra effort that a learner makes may in fact induce more aspiration than is usual to him, so it may even be audible on syllables without strong stress. Pupils can have the absence of aspiration in English after s pointed out to them, and can then

45

try to produce the same effect while imagining though not actually having pronounced the s. They may also be told to 'make something more like' the corresponding *voiced* plosive initially (b d g); this works well in true initial position, where English b d g are usually not fully voiced, but it will not apply medially as there b d g do get fully voiced in English.

For most Indian, many Far Eastern and some other languages opposition between strong aspiration and non-aspiration is incorporated structurally in each sound system. For learning such languages there is nothing for it but to work until mastery over the two kinds of voice onset (immediate and delayed) has been gained. It will help to think of the aspirated plosives as being p t k followed by h, so as to concentrate on aspirating them a great deal. In a sense which does not apply to European languages, then, the question of voice onset timing and therefore aspiration is essential to the proper pronunciation of such languages.

Full voicing

The English tendency is for voicing to die away during 'voiced' plosives and fricatives in word-final, pre-pausal position so that they sound at their very end more like their voiceless counterparts, but with weak breath force – so weak that the final consonant is almost imperceptible. This is therefore what English-speakers tend to do in their French – quite inappropriately since French final consonants following a vowel are all fully voiced (exceptions are found regionally, e.g. Alsace, Canada). It requires the greatest concentration to manage to keep the vocal cords in firm vibration for long enough at the end of a word which ends the group. The solution is to keep breathing out strongly and to make a point of maintaining voicing *until after the consonant has been finally released*; this 'overvoicing' can often be heard from French speakers and sounds like a vestigial vocalic offglide of central or indeterminate quality.

A diagram will make clear the difference between English and French usage: Eng. 'it shows' is compared with Fr. 'cette chose' for the behaviour of a group-final (pre-pausal) consonant. The vertical lines represent the beginning and end of the final fricative.

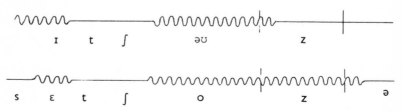

English-speakers soon manage to produce the right effect once or twice in succession when paying conscious attention, but that is quite another matter from achieving this very different vocal cord behaviour habitually and without thinking. Persistent overvoicing is not the long-term solution as excessive voice after the release of a consonant gives the impression of a vowel sound in its own right, forming another syllable, and though this is normal in Southern forms of French, it could hardly be put forward as the model for the English learner. Nevertheless any overvoicing is more 'French' than the weak and incomplete voicing that is typically English.

A number of other languages are similar to French in this whole matter. The full voicing of these final consonants is permanently troublesome for Slav, Germanic and all Anglo-Saxon speakers.

Pitch variation

The rise and fall of the voice is determined by changes in the frequency of vibration of the vocal cords, corresponding closely to differences of perceived pitch of sounds created by this vibration; higher pitch correlates with more rapid vibration of the vocal cords, lower pitch with slower vibration. The vocal cords are inside the larynx and pitch variation results from activity there, so the topic is dealt with at this point.

There are no observations on the subject of intonation (the rise and fall of the voice in connected speech) that would have special relevance for speakers of English as mother tongue: they, like everyone else, need to direct their attention to this important parameter of a spoken language and incorporate its features into their own performance. For the very young, for the more naive learner, and for those whose study time is limited, straightforward imitation of a good model may be all that is wanted. Particularly in this matter, adequate repetition by the teacher (see p. 13) when demonstrating an intonation pattern or contour is important, then insistence on its imitation. Recordings are useful here because of the mechanical repetition they can provide; of course all linguistic features get repeated when a recording is replayed, but intonation is one which is easily caught by the learner – indeed after listening a number of times to a recorded phrase it is really quite hard to reproduce it oneself with any *other* intonation. But accuracy of reproduction by the pupil is only part of the story: the problem for him is to find out what is typical, what is essential about a pattern or tune, and under what circumstances it would be used; then he has to produce it when wanted. It will be for the teacher to link the parameter of intonation with other parameters such as stress (if relevant), with word structure and with points of grammar and syntax.

47

During a course there may not be time to introduce a systematic treatment of intonational features, possibly with the help of some form of notation, or it may be judged unsuitable to present intonation for its own sake rather than treat it incidentally. But in any case the teacher should remain on the look-out for two things: any typical intonation patterns of the foreign language that the learner fails initially to reproduce from imitation, and any characteristic usages that the learner brings from his mother tongue which sound incongruous and 'wrong' when introduced into the foreign language; and he should by appropriate means bring these points to the learner's attention.

3.4   Tongue activity

For all new, unfamiliar articulations the speech organs have to be trained to get into unaccustomed positions and perform unusual actions. A teacher, who needs to know just what is required in each case, can often obtain from books the information he wants (see Bibliography, pp. 98–100). If it is not available in this form, he should do his best to get at the facts by asking other people or, better still, by noticing things for himself. When it comes to teaching a new articulation to his students, he should put into operation whatever methods he finds or expects to find successful (see pp. 26–8 for some teaching techniques and procedures).

Dentality

The tip and blade of the tongue, perhaps the most mobile and sensitive part of the whole vocal mechanism, is used in languages extensively for forming some of their most frequently occurring consonants. The tip can contact various points facing it, in particular the back of the upper front teeth, and the gums behind them known as the alveolar ridge; most languages make use predominantly of either the one or the other of these two main contact points. But Indian languages in particular make much use of both, and in some cases of a third, for establishing oppositions that they utilise for making distinctions between words. Speakers of most other languages have difficulty in using more than one contact point for the tip of the tongue, and those who use only one naturally have difficulty in not using it but using only the other.

The articulations for t d n l in English are all formed with the more retracted contact (apart from a few individuals) and are termed 'alveolar', meaning with contact against the alveolar ridge. The more advanced contact, called 'dental', is used for the corresponding sounds in all Romance and all Slav languages and thus in French, Spanish, Italian and Russian, which comprise the majority of the languages that English-speaking people most often learn as foreign languages. Only German among the most commonly studied languages has sounds that can be articulated with the retracted contact used in English, though this applies to most but not all of its speakers, mainly in the North. It follows that in learning to speak German the English person does not need to do anything in particular about t d n and l (as far as contact point is concerned), whereas for any of the other languages mentioned he does.

It is merely a matter of getting the tongue sufficiently forward in the mouth so that the advanced contact is made. It should be pointed out that there is for the English-speaker nothing unusual in so forward a position as such: the English TH-sounds, as in *thin* θɪn, *this* ðɪs, have the tongue touching the teeth, but loosely since these are fricatives with the breath coming through continuously. All that is necessary is to make firm contact at that point, thus checking the flow of air. Here it may be noted that this is precisely what is done whenever t d n or l precedes θ or ð, whether within a word as in *eighth* ɛɪtθ, *width* wɪdθ or wɪtθ, *tenth* tɛnθ, *health* hɛlθ, or by juxtaposition of separate words. A little experimenting under careful guidance should enable every pupil to find the right place for dental t d, and once the habit has been firmly fixed by plenty of practice, it will extend to cover n and l also without any need to give them separate attention.

It is well worth getting the dental sounds right: they are collectively of very high frequency in a language so the 'foreign' sensation is almost continuous, and this is of great psychological value to the learner, see p. 21. Furthermore, for moderate initial pains complete authenticity is permanently achieved.

Consonant combinations

Agglomerations of consonants, whether by consonant clusters occurring in the body of words or by juxtaposition in connected speech, are always liable to cause problems of articulation, in the first instance whenever the particular combination is unfamiliar to the speaker, and ultimately in any case whenever the sheer complication of successive movements and the speed of their execution taxes the skill and dexterity of every performer. Facility greater than that already possessed by a speaker can always be acquired by further practice. The technique is simply to rehearse whatever sequence of consonants or involving consonants is to be learnt, first slowly enough to get the succession of movements right, then with gradually increasing speed until greater skill has been obtained.

English-speakers to whom specific *initial* consonant clusters appear to be presenting special difficulty can often be brought to articulate them successfully by the device of juxtaposing *English* words in such a way as to bring about the combination that is wanted, then, after some rehearsal of the whole sequence, *starting* articulating at the appropriate point in the middle so that the combination concerned gets performed from an initial start. Thus the Russian sequence ʃtʃ, as in щи ʃtʃi, is found simpler after saying 'push-chair' (though it should be noted that the Russian combination commonly reduces to ʃʃ, but the English one cannot), German initial ts as in *zehn* is no further problem after 'not so' nor the tsv of *zwischen* after 'cat's fish', German pf as in *Pfeil* is easy after 'Cup Final', and similarly for other combinations.

However, it should be noted that not all juxtaposed consonants have to be pronounced in succession as they stand: each language has its own ways of making sequences of movements on occasion easier to execute than they would otherwise be, either by leaving out, (not pronouncing) a consonant, often the middle one of three ('elision', see Glossary), or by articulating a consonant in a way that makes it in some respect more like one of its neighbours ('assimilation', see Glossary), thus avoiding some more complicated sequence of movements. As pupils become more fluent the processes and tendencies that operate in their respective target language should be brought to their notice, and the teacher should see they incorporate them into their own pronunciation of the language.

Diphthongisation

There is a universal tendency for speakers to carry over their mother-tongue habits to their attempts at pronouncing foreign languages. This means that they will be inclined in the first place to identify non-native, previously unknown sounds with sounds they already know, and to pronounce accordingly; thus English-speakers may begin by replacing German ç by ʃ and German x by k. Furthermore, they will be influenced by the arrangement or pattern of sounds – the phonological structure – of the mother tongue and carry over habits formed by that pattern, so that they tend to mispronounce anything based on and conforming to a different pattern. If a certain vowel quality, or one very like it, occurs only *long* in their own language, they will be inclined to make it long in the target language even though it should be pronounced short. If a certain vowel quality, or one like it, never occurs at the end of a word or group in their own language, they will have difficulty in producing that quality in word- or group-final position, even though they may be capable of producing it satisfactorily in other positions. The tendency on the part of English-speaking people to diphthongise certain non-English vowels in certain positions is accounted for by the factors outlined above.

The non-English vowels most likely to be (incorrectly) diphthongised by English-speakers are of the type e and o, namely half-close front and half-close back vowels (see Diagram 3, p. 96) such as occur in a great many languages including French and German. The tendency is strongest when these vowels should be sounded long, and when they occur in final position, or both. The mispronunciation consists in beginning the sound from a too open tongue position and gliding during the syllable to a closer one, accompanied by an increase of lip-rounding in the case of o, thus producing an audible change of quality. The way to set about correcting it is to ensure that a close enough position is taken up right from the start of the sound, with no raising of the jaw or increased rounding of the lips (for o) visible during its production.

Those speakers of English who do not have a diphthongal pronunciation of the vowels in *day* and *go* naturally do not tend to diphthongise the vowels in question (though they may have other difficulties with them); they include speakers of regional varieties of English in Scotland, Wales and the North-East of England.

In final position a vowel may get diphthongised even when it should be made short: this is due to the English-speaker's difficulty in uttering most *short* vowels *finally*. Thus Fr. *aller* tends to be sounded more like Eng. *allay* than like Eng. *alley*, and It. *cade*, *otto* like Eng. *car day*, *Otto*. Notice how French words used in English take on these diphthongal vowels, as in *fiancé(e)*, *matinée*, *Bordeaux*, and many others.

Even vowels that should be pronounced more open, and short, may get diphthongised, as when Fr. *très* is made to rhyme with Eng. *tray*. Notice the anglicised versions of, for instance, *chef d'oeuvre*, *après ski*, *eau de cologne*, pronounced ʃɛɪ d ɜvr, æprɛɪ ski, əʊ də kələʊn, and compare Fr. ʃe (or ʃɛ) d œvr, apre ski, o d kɔlɔɲ.

Quite a separate diphthongising tendency may get carried over to vowels of the type i̯ and u̯ (see Diagram 3, p. 96) by those speakers who tend to diphthongise their English vowels in *me*, *do*. The correction of this tendency, for the target language, should be based on an insistence by the teacher on really close front and close back qualities right from the start of the two sounds.

51

Velarisation

Tendencies analogous to the foregoing affect English-speakers who accompany the lateral articulation and tongue tip contact of l with bunching up of the back of the tongue body towards the soft palate; this produces the auditory effect known as 'dark' or 'velarised l' (also found in Russian and in Turkish). Notice that not all English-speakers have 'dark l' in their speech – Irish, Welsh, some Northern English and some Scots typically have only 'clear' or 'non-velarised l'; other speakers lack a truly 'clear' l, notably some Scots and many Americans.

Of the most frequently studied foreign languages only Russian possesses any l that could be called 'dark'. To pronounce other languages well, the English-speaker with 'dark l' throughout his speech, or before a consonant or finally, has the problem of articulating a lateral consonant while bunching up the *front* of the tongue body. The teacher can help by demonstrating and drawing attention to the required quality of sound, and by insisting on the unfamiliar position that will produce this.

3.5 Influence of English spelling conventions

Occasionally an English mistake of pronunciation can be ascribed directly to the influence exerted by letters that in *English* spelling represent sounds which would be wrong in the context.

A typical case is where the letter *r* following a vowel letter, though not itself pronounced as r (and in a sense *because* it would not be so pronounced, in the speech of all 'R-droppers', see p. 58), is taken to indicate a *long vowel preceding it*. This is because of the common digraphic (vowel letter + *r*) representation of certain long vowels in English, notably *ar* for ɑ as in *hard*, *or* for ɔ as in *cord*, also *er*, *ir*, *ur* for ɜ as in *fern*, *girl*, *turn*. The matter of learning to articulate the r before another consonant, as in Fr. *parc*, *porte*, Ger. *Wort*, *Wurm*, Sp. or It. *parco*, *porta*, will have to be tackled separately by these speakers in any event, but the lengthening of the vowel in such words is likely to be due to a misunderstanding and directly to the influence of this particular English spelling convention.

Another instance is where letters associated with voiced sounds in English – and indeed in other spelling systems – are inevitably taken to stand for these in final position and so are pronounced too weakly, that is with the weak articulation used *finally* in these sounds in English – though not in fact with much voicing. Now in German and other Germanic languages, also in Slav languages, the distribution of voiced plosives and fricatives being restricted to *non*-final positions, it is the corresponding voiceless sounds (with strong breath force) that regularly replace them in word-final position, though the conventional spelling continues to suggest voiced sounds to the English eye. The use of a phonetic notation acts as a valuable reminder of the true state of affairs; a categorical statement is needed from the teacher to the effect that e.g. Ger. *wird* and *Wirt* sound *identical*, that *Mund* has the sound of *munter*, not of *Munde*, and so forth; and there should be systematic drilling in producing words *listed in their ordinary spelling* while using the correct sounds. In German the letter *s*, sounded (when standing singly) only as z initially but only as s finally, gives particular trouble in masculine genitive singulars; phrases of the type *des Mannes, eines Tages, dieses Mädchens* (dɪzəs mætçəns) need assiduous rehearsal. A way of bringing this last point home at an early stage, without resorting to phonetic symbols, is to *double* the final *s*'s of ordinary spelling and write up a few examples thus: *dess Manness* and so forth.

Specially disconcerting is the occurrence in German of voiceless articulations, contrary to the apparent implication of the spelling, medially even before another *voiced* consonant, as in *endlich* ɛntlɪç, *Liebling* lɪplɪŋ, *widmen* vɪtmən, *Ereignis* ɛr'aiknɪs.

3.6 Inventory of English-speakers' principal mispronunciations of other languages

(the letters after each item relate to the Categories described on p. 31)

1 Diphthongisation of some vowels, notably e o i u, especially finally. B
2 Lengthening of certain vowels, notably i u, especially finally. C
3 Centralisation of certain vowels under weak stress, especially i a. B
4 Fronting of u. D
5 Absence of lip-rounding. B/D
6 Eng. r for other types of r-sound. B
7 Omission of r finally or before a consonant. C/D
8 Velarisation of l finally or before a consonant. B/D
9 Aspiration of p t k, especially before a stressed vowel. D
10 Alveolar contact for t d n. B
11 Heavy stress on some syllables. D
12 Fall-Rise and Low Rise intonation patterns. C/D
(Nos. 2, 9, 10, 11 would not be incorrect for German.)

Outstanding additional tendencies or difficulties in pronouncing 5 particular languages

French

1 Stress-timing for syllable-timing. **D**
2 Replacements and confusions: u for y, ɔ̃ for ã, w for ɥ, *le/la*. **A**
3 Front rounded vowels (y ø œ) as such. **B**
4 Close vowels (i u y e o ø) not close enough. **B/D**
5 Insertion of nasal consonant after a nasal vowel before another consonant, e.g. pɔ̃mp for pɔ̃p (*pompe*), ʃãnt for ʃãt (*chante*). **C/D**
6 Voiced plosives (b d g) and fricatives (v z ʒ) unvoiced finally, also initially. **D**
7 Failure to unvoice l r finally after voiceless consonant, as in *quatre* katr, *peuple* pœpl. **C**
8 Elisions usually not made. **C/D**

German

1 Replacements and confusions:
   u for y, ʊ for ʏ, ə/ər finally; **A**
   o too open (ɔ) before r, e too open (æ) before r; **C**
   z for s finally; **B**
   ʃ for ç, k for x (elementary stage). **B**
2 Front rounded vowels (y ʏ ø œ): y ø not front and not rounded, ʏ too like y, œ too long. **B**
3 ç not front enough, x not back enough (at later stage). **D**
4 Distribution of long/short vowels. **C/D**
5 Reduced forms of articles, especially *den*, *der*, *dem*. **C/D**
6 Final plosives and fricatives voiced under influence of ordinary spelling, especially final -*d* and final -*s*, as in *Bad*, *stand*, *des*, *als*. **B**
7 Failure to sustain High Level pitch (for incomplete utterances). **C**

Italian

1 Doubled consonants not long enough. **B**
2 Single consonants sometimes not short enough (at later stage). **C**
3 Lengthened vowels not long enough. **B/D**
4 e too open before r, as in *sera*. **C**
5 a varied (Eng. æ ɑ ə) according to position. **C**

Russian

1 Palatalisation, especially of t d. **B**
2 Position of strong stress in words and sentences. **C/D**

Spanish

1 Intervocalic weakening of b d g from plosive to fricative articulations. **B**

4 Teaching speakers of other languages to pronounce English

4.1 Which kind of English?

Most people no doubt embark on their study of the English language (as of any language not their own) without ever having been in a position to choose between alternative models of pronunciation: what they found themselves obliged to accept will have been determined by such factors as their own whereabouts at the time, the teaching tradition in the area, and teacher availability in the given instance. Few beginners are able actually to choose between attending one school or institution or another; this is the case whether a variety of teaching establishments in fact exist in their own country, or even supposing they might consider setting out for other parts of the English-speaking world. However, some observations on the subject of different kinds of English may be relevant here, not only for these latter minorities but also for the considerable number who, though unable to exercise a choice, are inclined at times to worry over the matter and wonder whether they will subsequently find themselves in any way at a disadvantage through becoming exponents of one variety of English rather than another.

The first need is to reassure the learner and to encourage a sense of proportion: all types of English have far more in common than they have divergencies. English *as such* has numerous characteristics that will engage the attention and best efforts of every foreign learner, of whatever nationality; the differences between types – whether of a phonetic nature or of vocabulary or usage – though quite apparent, really do not count a great deal in comparison.

The second requirement is information: the learner, once in possession of the facts, is in a good position to decide for himself whether he should modify his current pronunciation in some respect and if so in what direction; or alternatively, to decide to make no change and in that case to stop worrying.

The two principal varieties of world English are of course those spoken in North America (Canada and the United States) and in Britain. Except for some special reason, the foreign learner would be well advised to model his speech on one of these two – though, conversely, it would be sensible for a person emigrating to, say, Australia to aim for Australian rather than any other kind of English: the general intention should surely be to fit in as well as possible to one's environment. But it should be remembered that a non-native speaker of English is far more likely to be conspicuous *as a foreigner* than as a speaker of some variety of English not native to the locality. So let the average learner concentrate first on eradicating from his speech those features that make him most conspicuous as a foreigner, in whatever part of the world, while at the same time mastering the features that apply to all forms of English. Having got his priorities right and done these things, he can then devote some attention to regional differences within the English-speaking world. By the time he has reached the advanced level where these aspects become more relevant for him he may very well be capable of adapting his speech consciously to his environment and so becoming to some extent bilingual in English, speaking more like an American when in America and less like one when in Britain. To be completely successful at this may be beyond all but a few, but since in any case some unconscious approximation to the speech one hears around one is likely, indeed inevitable, there is much to be said for a systematic and informed approach to the whole question in order that the end result may be the more satisfactory.

From the foregoing remarks addressed to the learner of English it will be clear what the advice to a teacher should be. The *native* exponent of a given accent is bound to be exemplifying that accent continually to his pupils, and it would be unrealistic to expect them to acquire from him any other form of speech than his own: it is quite beyond the capacity of an American teacher (even if he wished) to teach any form of 'British' English, and conversely. However, it can happen that a teacher with a marked regional accent of some kind will make concessions, consciously or unconsciously, to a less marked variety at least for the purpose of *demonstrating* the pronunciation; and the better informed he is as to the nature of the various phonetic differences, the more likely he will be to achieve a consistent and integrated performance and so be of greatest help as a model for his pupils. Moreover in concentrating, rightly, on what would make his pupils conspicuous as *foreign* speakers of English, he will avoid giving undue importance to matters involving regional variation, at least unless or until they are so advanced as to be judged ready for this kind of thing. But then it would not be inappropriate for a teacher on occasion to point out that though he himself was to be heard pronouncing in a given manner, he would (for whatever reason) recommend his pupils not to imitate him in that particular usage.

Now in the case of the teacher for whom English is a foreign language, he will in the course of his own study have come under influences of one kind or another, first and foremost his teacher(s), then of any English-speaking areas he may have visited or lived in, then of any media such as cinema, radio and television, disc or tape recording, where some variety of English has been spoken. If as a result of all this his own speech is something of a mixture, he can obtain information (from this book and elsewhere) that will enable him to sort out the phonetic differences and, if he so wishes, adopt or discard particular usages.

R-dropping

Quite the most noticeable and characteristic feature of pronunciation that distinguishes the two main varieties of world English is concerned with the relationship between the actual sounding of r and the occurrence of the letter r in English words as conventionally spelt. In the 'American' or 'Trans-Atlantic' type there is a one-to-one relationship between sound and spelling, meaning that wherever a letter r is found in spelling, there the sound is found pronounced. In the 'British' or 'Cis-Atlantic' type the sound of r is found pronounced *only when the immediately following sound is a vowel* (whether in the same or the next word) – that is, it is not articulated as r in positions before other consonant sounds or before pause, i.e. finally in a group.[1] In these positions the letter r has to be looked upon as combining with a preceding vowel letter to form a digraph representing jointly some particular vowel sound, e.g. *ar* may stand for ɑ, *ur* for ɜ, and so forth. Thus the letter r does not correspond to a pronounced consonant sound in all these cases, which form about one half of the total.

So as to see how this works out in practice, a passage of written English

[1] It must be pointed out at once that there are important exceptions both ways to this general statement, which in the above passage relating to 'Trans-Atlantic' would not describe the usage of many parts of the South and East of the United States, and in that relating to the British Isles is at variance with the usage of most speakers in Scotland, Ireland and the South-West of England, among others; in the parts just mentioned the usage is in fact reversed. Nevertheless the two different treatments of r as defined above are very widely associated with 'Trans-Atlantic' and 'Cis-Atlantic' respectively – so much so that a *non*-native speaker of English is almost certain to be 'placed' or identified with one or the other on the basis of this feature alone and possibly in disregard of other, contrary indications.

is shown below in which every letter *r* that is silent, i.e. not pronounced as
r, in 'R-dropping' parts of the English-speaking world is printed in
italics. Those *r*'s that are sounded only because the following word begins
with a vowel and no pause is made or is likely to be made, owing to a fairly
close grammatical connection between the two words, are shown with a
mark of linking. One italic *r* is bracketed to show an optional link. The
passage contains 46 *r*'s of which 27 are 'silent' (one optionally) and 19 are
pronounced as r (including 5 linking two words). It will be seen that over
half of all the *r*'s are italicised, the remainder corresponding to a pronounced r with *all* speakers.

Afte*r* listening one mo*r*ning to thei*r* effusions, M*r* Bennet
coolly obse*r*ved:
    'From all that I can collect by you*r* manne*r* of talking
you must be two of the silliest gi*r*ls in the country. I have
suspected it some time, but I am now convinced.'
    Cathe*r*ine was disconce*r*ted, and made no answe*r*; but
Lydia, with pe*r*fect indifference, continued to express
he*r* admiration of Captain Carte(*r*), and he*r* hope of seeing
him in the cou*r*se of the day, as he was going the next
mo*r*ning to London.
    'I am astonished, my dea*r*,' said M*r*s Bennet, 'that you
should be so ready to think you*r* own children silly. If I
wished to think slightingly of anybody's children it should
not be of my own, howeve*r*.'
    'If my children a*r*e silly, I must hope to be always
sensible of it.'
    'Yes; but as it happens, they a*r*e all of them very cleve*r*.'
    'This is the only point, I flatte*r* myself, on which we do
not agree. I had hoped that ou*r* sentiments coincided in
every pa*r*ticula*r*, but I must so fa*r* diffe*r* from you as to
think ou*r* two youngest daughte*r*s uncommonly foolish.'

Now many foreign learners acquire without much difficulty what is for
them a new consonant articulation for use in English, but for those who
continue to use their native R-sound in English – one of the most noticeable features of a 'foreign accent' – it can be pointed out that by taking
some 'R-dropping' variety of English as their model they could cut out
quite half of their mispronunciations by simply not articulating *any*
consonant sound in those places where the letter is written but the sound
can be dropped.

An understanding of the 'rule' operating here will enable the foreign speaker to adopt some *consistent* usage. Though variability between words and from one moment to the next probably would not interfere with understanding, it can at times be disconcerting, perhaps momentarily confusing, and is bound to give a foreign effect. (This applies to inconsistency with regard to other features also.)

Some further differences between 'Cis-Atlantic' and 'Trans-Atlantic' accents of English also involve *distribution* of sounds. Three of the more striking cases with vowels are as follows: (1) The Y-sound as in *you* is not pronounced before the vowel u (as in *you*) in certain cases in 'Trans-Atlantic' speech where it is pronounced in 'Cis-Atlantic'. Compare Trans/Cis pronunciation of *due*, *dew* which in Trans can rhyme with *do*, not with *few*; and of *duty* which can rhyme with *booty*, not with *beauty*.

(2) Many words that have 'long A' (as in *calm*) in 'Cis-Atlantic' have the quality of 'short A' (as in *cat*) in 'Trans-Atlantic'. Compare Trans/Cis pronunciation of *bath*, *past*, *half*, *can't*, and notice that the Trans vowel can sound quite *long*. (In the British Isles as a whole the usage is not homogeneous with these words: in the North of England the 'short A' (really pronounced short) occurs in many words that have 'long A' in other areas; conversely in Scotland a vowel resembling 'long A' is used in some words that have 'short A' elsewhere, e.g. *have*.)

(3) Speakers of English in Britain – whatever different shades of vowel qualities they may have – generally sort into three separate categories the words *calm*, *long*, *cause*, and they know to which of the three any other word, such as *bomb*, *dog*, *lost*, belongs. Most speakers in America possess only two vowel distinctions in this quality area and so have all words in a third category distributed among the other two, so to speak – but somewhat unpredictably and with variations between speakers.

Distribution differences apart from the foregoing are fairly insignificant. Pronouncing dictionaries should be consulted and compared for information on the sounds in any given word.

Differences of quite another kind, namely quality characteristics of several individual vowels in each system, also distinguish Trans from Cis – as they distinguish any variety of English from any other. For detailed information on all such matters, books that have been written on pronunciation of each type should be referred to, and available recordings of spoken English studied.

In this book all phonetically transcribed material is in conformity with 'Cis-Atlantic' as opposed to 'Trans-Atlantic' sound sequences and distribution; it also illustrates a form of speech of a particular kind, as will be described below.

Regarding varieties of English speech generally, the foreign learner is recommended to listen to native speakers wherever they may be from and wherever he may be; he will derive great benefit from cultivating his powers of observation and adding to his experience in countless ways. To try to shut one's ears to accents of any particular kind on the grounds that one might not wish to adopt them would surely not be making the best use of one's opportunities.

'Received Pronunciation'

This term, which has been current among specialists for over a century, is used by them to refer to a certain accent of British English. They call it RP when they speak or write about it, and now rarely use the expression in its full form 'received pronunciation'. The word 'received' in this sense is quite old-fashioned and would not be widely understood today. It meant 'socially acceptable', 'received in good society', and could refer to speech, dress or various forms of behaviour. It was often used negatively, i.e. to point out that something was not or would not be received 'in the best circles'.

Although RP *is* an accent (if by accent one means 'way of speaking'), people with RP are sometimes referred to as speaking 'without an accent'; this of course means without a *regional* accent. This draws attention to what is its unique characteristic: all other accents of Britain carry regional connotations. A speaker with any other accent may or may not be identified as belonging to one social class or another, but in either case he is sure to exhibit some regional features in his speech. RP alone does not do this, but does connect the user with the upper levels of society. In the minds of people elsewhere RP is linked broadly with London and the South-East of England, mainly because it shares 'R-dropping' with other accents of that region; but in fact RP is acquired by many born and brought up in other parts.

The present-day situation has evolved gradually in four main ways: (1) Formerly, hundreds of years ago, every speaker must have used the speech of his region; but some degree of standardisation would have tended to occur early under the influence of London, the capital and seat of government, with the presence of the monarchy and the social prestige of Court circles.

(2) Dissemination of the cultured speech of the capital was brought about firstly by the fact that well-to-do families lived for most of the time on their country estates, often at some distance from London where they spent only part of the year; and then by the fact that sons of these families

traditionally followed callings such as the Church, the Army and the Law, so barristers, clergymen and army officers, whose speech could have been widely heard by relatively large numbers (before the days of the cinema, radio and television) lent social prestige to their natural way of speaking.

(3) Then came the fashion for boys to be sent away from home to boarding-schools which, besides offering a classical education of a good academic standard, caused their pupils' speech to become ever more homogeneous as a result of boys from various parts of the country being thrown together at an impressionable age.

(4) In the nineteenth century the Industrial Revolution made some men wealthy quite rapidly and for the first time. By sending their sons to one of these by now more numerous boarding-schools, since they could now afford the fees, many who themselves had a regional speech were able to ensure that the next generation grew up without it, thereby improving their status while obtaining 'a good education' which meant manners and social graces as well as book learning. The female line, while not imbibing so much Latin and Greek, developed their social graces and picked up the favoured accent with equal if not greater facility.

In days gone by, culture and education were readily accessible only to a small and privileged class, so terms such as 'cultured speech' and 'educated speech' came to be synonymous with 'upper-class speech'. Over the last hundred years education and culture have become increasingly available to ever wider sections of the community and for a long time now people speaking with accents other than RP have not necessarily lacked advanced education or culture. Conversely, however, enough of the old historical association does remain for it to be taken for granted that anyone speaking *with* an RP accent will possess a certain degree of culture and sophistication and will have received a certain type and standard of education.

But an important development of only about the last twenty or thirty years has been the changing attitude to questions of accent. With class distinctions breaking down and with many now non-existent, a variety of accents can be heard from people in almost all walks of life, and there is far less pressure to conform. This is also true for those who would traditionally have been RP speakers: regional (non-RP) influences are beginning to be quite noticeable among most of the younger generation everywhere, and within a few decades it seems likely that exponents of a strict RP will be hard to find.

On the other hand, though RP itself has always been the accent of a small minority, it is observable that today a large number of others speak with a close approximation to it. This is probably due more to a tendency towards standardisation generally than to any exceptional social prestige attaching nowadays to RP.

There is no good reason for advising the foreign learner of English coming under 'Cis-Atlantic' influence *not* to take RP as his general model, but it is not very important nor even perhaps desirable that he should acquire it to perfection – if indeed this were possible. One advantage to the foreigner is that it is easy to learn *about* RP because it has been very fully described in the many books that have been written about it and exemplify it; it is in fact not at all easy to find adequate descriptions of other accents.

The phonetic features of RP (apart from 'R-dropping' which RP shares with many other accents) reside mainly in shades of vowel quality. In the case of certain vowels there are quite crucial, if often subtle, quality differences between RP and non-RP; with other vowels there is little if any difference – and indeed in the case of some there can be greater difference between speakers *within* RP than between an RP and a non-RP vowel quality. In any event, RP vowels have changed and are changing over the years, as with every other accent; also, at any one time perceptible differences exist between the various age groups.

4.2   Influence of English spelling

It is a commonplace that the conventional spelling of English is inconsistent, and therefore unreliable as a guide to the proper sequences of sounds to be articulated in speaking. At the same time it has to be accepted that large numbers of foreigners in each generation approach English through the medium of the printed word and it is inevitable that they should all be powerfully influenced by it in spite of the warnings of its irregularities that they are sure to receive from their teachers – and indeed are bound to notice for themselves as soon as they try to learn to *spell*. The effect on their pronunciation is quite specific: quite apart from faulty pronunciations of the kind that could be predicted of every foreign speaker in any event, namely those due to the different articulatory habits acquired from his mother tongue, acquaintance with English spelling induces a whole crop of mispronunciations of a quite separate kind, namely those that involve aiming at, and consequently uttering, sequences of articulations *other than* the sequences that should properly be aimed at for a correct pronunciation of the English words and sentences. The sequences they aim to produce are of course ones that are first suggested by the spelling and are then only too liable to become habitual.

The problem is to know what to do about this state of affairs in so far as it has a bearing on the teaching and learning of pronunciation. We are not here concerned with how to teach English spelling, where training of the visual memory is what is mainly involved; this will prove more effective if undertaken in some systematic way such as by drawing attention to regularities in the patterning and by separating out anything forming exceptions to these. Now a systematic approach to the articulations of spoken English is equally desirable; but the point to note is that the spelling of written English and the pronunciation of sequences of English sounds are two different matters, so different that they are best tackled separately and not, in the first instance, the one in terms of the other. When the time comes to expound the relationship between the two, namely when a framework for the phenomena of pronunciation has been firmly established as such, it will then be found easier and better to describe the spelling of words in terms of their sounds rather than to attempt to teach the sounds from the spellings.

Letter values

But even if all exceptions and anomalies were absent from English spelling, the English spelling conventions are in many cases at variance with those of other languages that use basically the same roman alphabet of letters. This in itself can cause some disruption in the early stages of learning to speak English, and the temptation must be resisted from the outset to equate letters used in English with the values they have in other orthographies. The articulation of r wherever r appears in the spelling is an instance of this, see p. 58.

The best solution is systematic exposition of the English sounds for their own sake, with later a systematic study of the letters that are most often used for these sounds in ordinary spelling; the exceptions then gradually fall into place. Even when some familiarity with the printed word has preceded any real work on pronunciation (regrettably, in view of the result of this on the learner) it may well be best to lay aside such knowledge temporarily and go first for establishing the sounds of the language in their own right.

No letter for shwa

One of the features of the English vowel system is that it contains one sound possessing the unique attribute of being unable to bear strong stress, unlike all the other vowels. (This is the characteristic feature of the letter of the Hebrew alphabet – shwa, which in recent years has come to be used as a technical term of phonetic description.) Since this occurs in a high proportion of all the weakly stressed syllables in connected speech, it follows that it is one of the commonest vowel sounds in the language.

This vowel has a 'central' quality, deriving from its intermediate tongue position (see p. 73) which is often hard to produce for people whose mother tongue has no central vowel, and which they will need to learn. The phonetic symbol for a typical central vowel in any language is ə, and this is found in all the sets of symbols that have been and are used for English (see p. 92). It is also regularly used in the transcription of French and of German, both of which have a central vowel that shares with the English one the attribute of being unable to bear strong stress. But the most striking thing about the English shwa, and what causes the foreign speaker the greatest trouble, is the fact that the roman alphabet not only does not have a special letter to stand for it, but *no one roman letter* covers all its occurrences (as the letter *e* does in French and in German). On the contrary, each of the vowel letters of the roman alphabet (*a, e, i, o, u*) can be found corresponding to occurrences of ə in spoken English, and so can a number of combinations of letters (such as *ar, er, or, our, ure*). The following words illustrate this: *woman* 'wʊmən, *about* ə'baʊt; *agent* 'ɛɪdʒənt, *gentlemen* 'dʒɛntlmən; *horrible* 'hɒrəbl; *method* 'mɛθəd, *correct* kə'rɛkt; *circus* 'sɜkəs, *surround* sə'raʊnd; *grammar* 'græmə; *brother* 'brʌðə; *doctor* 'dɒktə; *famous* 'fɛɪməs; *colour* 'kʌlə; *figure* 'fɪgə. The result of course is that in a great many cases the foreign speaker – even though he may be quite capable of getting his tongue into the right position and so of producing the right quality of sound – does not do so because he does not *try* to do so since he cannot tell from the spelling when shwa is the sound he should pronounce; so he proceeds to utter some other vowel that the spelling suggests to him. For weakly stressed positions this is likely to be one of the other short vowels where in fact ə should be used: the letter *a* will suggest æ, *o* will invite ɒ, and so on; thus it is common to hear *England* given the vowel of *land*, *Europe* made to rhyme with *drop*, the last syllable of *famous* sounding like *moose*, and similarly in countless other words. Of course quite often the foreign speakers will introduce wrongly not other short vowels of English but outright vowels from his own language that have no place in English at all, but have nevertheless been suggested by the spelling; thus Eng. *suppose* can be heard from a French speaker sounding exactly like the corresponding French word – sypoz instead of sə'pəʊz.

If a person is unable to produce a central vowel quality this must first be learnt, probably most easily just by imitation. But a separate and continuing problem is to form speech habits with sequences of sounds, including ə, in the right places while the English spelling continues to lead astray. Phonetic notation is a good antidote and reminder: thus 'ɪŋglənd, 'jʊərəp, 'fɛɪməs; a pronouncing dictionary should always be at hand for consulting on which sounds occur in a given word.

Now it would be possible, supposing there were a letter for shwa in the English alphabet, to show the distribution of the sound in all words whose pronunciation is invariable; thus for example *photograph* would have the letter in the second syllable, while *photographer* would have it in the first, third and fourth syllables. In the absence of such a letter, it would be possible for teaching purposes, though awkward, to deal with ə occurrences in such words by marking the orthography in some way. But devices such as underlining or ringing vowel letters of an orthographic text are in danger of giving *prominence* to the places concerned, and for rendering shwa that is just what is not wanted! A vertical line through the letter, as if crossing it out, might work better. But in any case, all this would hardly begin to deal with a further problem – that of connected speech, where many common words (which, in isolation, would be sounded with other vowels – ones that are indeed suggested by their ordinary spelling) are likely to be sounded with ə (see Weak forms, p. 74 below).

4.3   Management of the breath

Unequal amounts of energy or effort are expended on syllables when they are uttered in sequences. When a markedly greater effort goes into pronouncing a syllable, it is said to be strongly stressed or simply 'stressed'. (The result is usually, though not invariably, to make the syllable concerned stand out from its neighbours and sound more prominent or 'louder'.) A language that has certain of its syllables pronounced with greater effort than the others as a necessary feature of every word or phrase is called a 'stress language'. The effort may fall regularly at the same point, for example on the first syllable, in all words having more than one syllable, or it may fall irregularly; the stress is termed either 'fixed' or 'free' accordingly. In words of one syllable the question of the place of stress does not arise, but in a sentence such words are either given a strong stress or not, depending on the sense to be conveyed and the usages of the language.

Stress and stress-timing

English is a stress language and its stress is free. This means that it will be necessary to know *where* stress falls in a word (of more than one syllable) before it can be pronounced properly. (It will also be necessary to know where strong stress would fall in a sentence before it could be accepted as usual English, or without perhaps giving an incorrect or unintended meaning to the sentence.) An English word should be learnt from the outset along with its stress, and should always be said with strong stress correctly placed. No learner should remain uncertain where the proper place is: any dictionary will supply the information, and he should get into the habit of consulting one – just as he would when wanting to know a word's meaning. There are alternative ways of stressing a number of English words but only one of these ways need be learnt and used, i.e. each word can always be said in the one way (but see p. 74 below). The advanced student can take note of any alternatives that exist, and study them with the help of a pronouncing dictionary.

But knowing where the stress ought to be placed is not the whole story: many foreign learners of English find difficulty in making the right syllable – or indeed any syllable – stand out enough (see p. 42). They need to get into the way of 'pushing' on some syllables, the strongly stressed ones, and of not pushing on others.

The role of a teacher in this matter of stress is, as usual, simply to insist that the stressing of a word or sentence, once the facts have been made known, be physically achieved by the speaker while actually speaking – in other words, to see to it that his manner of saying the word or sentence conveys the right stresses and no others, thus giving due importance to particular parts of his utterance, by the means proper to English, and so communicating the desired meaning.

An effective way of drawing the attention of a pupil to what is wanted, and of checking whether he has got the strong stressing of specific syllables under his control, is to invite him to accompany each stress, as he pronounces, by a firm, visible gesture such as a movement of the arm in time with each stress. English people themselves can often be observed, when speaking emphatically, to nod the head or make a gesture with the hand, in time with their strong stresses. For the speaker of a stress language the co-ordination of stress with other bodily movement presents no problem; any failure to do so, on the part of the non-English learner, gives a measure of the difficulty that stressing syllables strongly, and control over this, still holds for him.

Practice material can take the form of English words, classified in lists according to their stress pattern, each list giving a specific 'rhythm' due to the recurrence of the same pattern in each word. A few examples follow; for a fuller treatment see *A Practice Book of English Speech*, pp. 6–11.

	–ˈ– – –		ˌ– –ˈ– –
activity	æk'tɪvətɪ	*accidental*	ˌæksɪ'dɛntl
ambassador	æm'bæsədə	*beneficial*	ˌbɛnɪ'fɪʃl
consecutive	kən'sɛkjʊtɪv	*complication*	ˌkɒmplɪ'keɪʃn
democracy	dɪ'mɒkrəsɪ	*democratic*	ˌdɛmə'krætɪk
expenditure	ɪks'pɛndɪtʃə	*manufacture*	ˌmænjʊ'fæktʃə
unanimous	ju'nænɪməs	*understanding*	ˌʌndə'stændɪŋ

A group of learners can get valuable practice, together or singly, by saying lists of similarly stressed words aloud while marking the beat. One rhythm can be rehearsed for ten or fifteen seconds, then a different pattern taken. More rapid alternation between patterns follows, culminating in single examples of each pattern. The final stage is reached when a word is correctly pronounced when met in the body of a text or in connected speaking.

Short sentences can be constructed having the same rhythm as individual words, caused by the same succession of stressed and unstressed syllables spoken without a break. Thus for instance: *classification, not in the morning; etymological, just when I wanted you; originality, instead of telling him*, and so forth. The graded exercises described in the previous paragraph can be carried out equally effectively on sentences instead of words. Or the two types can be alternated.

A tendency is at work in the speaking of English (and some other languages) to have strongly stressed syllables succeed one another at approximately equal intervals of time, such as every half or other fraction of a second. So as to conform more closely to this pattern, a larger number of syllables (such as two or three) occurring between one stress and the next gets pronounced more rapidly than a lesser number of syllables (such as one or none at all) – though without disregarding completely the conditions affecting the structure of words, such as the number and nature of consonants at particular points, or the inherent length or shortness of vowels. In connected speech this results in continual variation in the rate at which syllables are being uttered, which gives the effect of speeding up and slowing down the speaking. This tendency is known as 'stress-timing'; English is a 'stress-timed' language. See p. 42 above for a description of the opposite tendency – 'syllable-timing', where any prominence or stress on individual syllables does not influence the pace of their articulation, which tends on the contrary to remain constant at a rate

68

of, say, 4 to 6 per second for as long as speaking continues uninterruptedly, that is until a speaker reaches the end of his sentence or deliberately inserts a pause.

Some practice material for English is set out below. Exercises 1–4 can be used for rehearsing the placing of strong stress at regular, rhythmic intervals, while a given number of weakly stressed syllables, e.g. one or two or three, falls between each stress. Variations in syllable rate become perceptible only when a sentence contains *varying* numbers of syllables between strong stresses. Any connected passage of English of course provides evidence of this, and opportunities for practising it, but an intermediate stage is exemplified in Exercises 5–6 which show some common sequences arranged systematically, e.g. one alternating with two, or two with three (syllables between successive stresses).

Stress practice

Sentences having an equal number of weakly stressed syllables between each strong stress

1 *One syllable*

Jack and Jill went up the hill
Tinker, tailor, soldier, sailor
Thirteen, fourteen, fifteen, sixteen
July the fifth at half past seven
Monday, Tuesday, Wednesday, Thursday, Friday
The curfew tolls the knell of parting day

2 *Two syllables*

Breakfast is ready, it's time to get up
Leave it to me and get on with your work
They live in the house at the end of the road
September, October, November, December
There was an old woman who lived in a shoe
A bird in the hand is worth two in the bush

3 *Three syllables*

Give it me this morning and I'll finish it by tea-time
Well, why didn't you say so when you came into the house?
There's nothing to be gained by demonstrations of hostility

4 *No syllables*

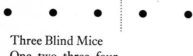

Three Blind Mice
One, two, three, four
Ships, planes, cars, trains
John Smith loves Jill Brown

The sentences on the page opposite in phonetic notation

1 *One syllable*

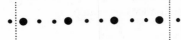

'dʒæk ənd 'dʒɪl wɛnt 'ʌp ðə 'hɪl
'tɪŋkə 'tɛɪlə 'səʊldʒə 'sɛɪlə
'θɜtin 'fɔtin 'fɪftin 'sɪkstin
dʒʊ'lʌɪ ðə 'fɪfθ ət 'haf pɑst 'sɛvn
'mʌndɪ 'tjuzdɪ 'wɛnzdɪ 'θɜzdɪ 'frʌɪdɪ
ðə 'kɜfju 'təʊlz ðə 'nɛl əv 'pɑtɪŋ 'dɛɪ

2 *Two syllables*

'brɛkfəst ɪz 'rɛdɪ ɪt s 'tʌɪm tə gɛt 'ʌp
'lɪv ɪt tə 'mi ən gɛt 'ɒn wɪð jɔ 'wɜk
ðɛɪ 'lɪv ɪn ðə 'hʌʊs ət ðɪ 'ɛnd əv ðə 'rəʊd
sɛp'tɛmbər ɒk'təʊbə nəʊ'vɛmbə dɪ'sɛmbə[1]
ðɛə 'wɒz ən əʊld 'wʊmən hu 'lɪvd ɪn ə 'ʃu
ə 'bɜd ɪn ðə 'hænd ɪz wɜθ 'tu ɪn ðə 'bʊʃ

3 *Three syllables*

'gɪv ɪt mi ðə'smɔnɪŋ ən ʌɪ l 'fɪnɪʃ ɪt bʌɪ 'tɪtʌɪm
wɛl 'wʌɪ dɪdnt ju 'sɛɪ səʊ wɛn ju 'kɛɪm ɪntə ðə 'hʌʊs
ðə z 'nʌθɪŋ tə bɪ 'gɛɪnd bʌɪ dɛməns'trɛɪʃnz əv hɒs'tɪlətɪ

4 *No syllables*

'θri 'blʌɪn 'mʌɪs
'wʌn 'tu 'θri 'fɔ
'ʃɪps 'plɛɪnz 'kɑz 'trɛɪnz
'dʒɒn 'smɪθ 'lʌvz 'dʒɪl 'brʌʊn

---

[1] Alternative pronunciations: səp'tɛmbə, nə'vɛmbə.

Sentences having an alternating number of weakly stressed syllables between strong stresses

5 *One and two syllables*

Raise your hand if you think you know what it means
Come and see what I've bought today for the children
I suppose you want me to bring it back in the morning

When she got there the cupboard was bare
Little Jack Horner sat in the corner
He put in his thumb and pulled out a plum

6 *Two and three syllables*

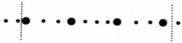

That was the difficulty, right from the start
When I asked if they wanted any, nobody answered
Most of the people in the house were delighted

Come into the garden and see what I've discovered
Nothing in the world would persuade me to receive them
The beginning of the end or the end of the beginning

5 *One and two syllables*

'reɪz jɔ 'hænd ɪf ju 'θɪŋk ju 'nəʊ wɒt ɪt 'minz
'kʌm ən 'si wɒt ʌɪ v 'bɒt tə'deɪ fə ðə 'tʃɪldrən
ʌɪ sə'pəʊz ju 'wɒnt mi tə 'brɪŋ ɪt 'bæk ɪn ðə 'mɔnɪŋ

'wɛn ʃi gɒt 'ðɛə ðə 'kʌbəd wəz 'bɛə
'lɪtl dʒæk 'hɔnə 'sæt ɪn ðə 'kɔnə
hi 'pʊt ɪn hɪz 'θʌm ənd 'pʊld ʌʊt ə 'plʌm

6 *Two and three syllables*

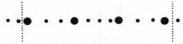

'ðæt wəz ðə 'dɪfəkltɪ 'rʌɪt frəm ðə 'stat
wɛn ʌɪ 'askt ɪf ðɛɪ 'wɒntɪd ɛnɪ 'nəʊbədɪ 'ansəd
'məʊst əv ðə 'pipl ɪn ðə 'hʌʊs wə dɪ'lʌɪtɪd

'kʌm ɪntə ðə 'gadn ənd 'si wɒt ʌɪ v dɪs'kʌvəd
'nʌθɪŋ ɪn ðə 'wɜld wʊd pə'swɛɪd mi tə rɪ'siv ðəm
ðə bɪ'gɪnɪŋ əv ðɪ 'ɛnd ɔ ðɪ 'ɛnd əv ðə bɪ'gɪnɪŋ

Centralisation

As a complementary phenomenon to strong stress on certain syllables
there is a tendency to expend little and ever less force on the other
syllables. As a result they get 'reduced': vowels get shortened and may
eventually be left out entirely, and whole syllables – consonants as well as
vowels – can 'drop out', not being pronounced at all. This is a
phenomenon observed frequently in the history of languages. Accompanying the shortening of vowels, and presumably due – as the shortening
is – to the weak breath force expended, we find the tendency for all the

articulating organs to be exerted less vigorously, and in particular for the tongue to move less in any direction towards more extreme positions, in the course of sequences of rapid articulatory movements, but instead to reach only, or to remain in, more intermediate, *central* positions in the mouth. In the case of English, centralisation – as this tendency is termed – has gone so far that truly central as well as some centralised (somewhat central) vowels form an integral part of the English system of vowel distinctions; and these are of very frequent occurrence in English words and sentences. The commonest of all, on which strong stress can (as it happens) never fall, is unrecorded in traditional orthography, so when to use it in pronouncing can only be learnt by other means. A person who studied English without ever having heard the language spoken might never discover the existence of this vowel. And the influence of ordinary spelling, and of the example of those (non-English speakers) who have been brought up exclusively on the spelling, is powerful enough to make the proper pronunciation of a weakly stressed central vowel (shwa, see p. 64), in the places where it should be used, continuously troublesome for the foreign learner. In addition to the many shwa syllables in words of more than one syllable (which can be looked up in a dictionary) referred to on pp. 65, 66, there are all the common monosyllables that have more than one pronunciation, including, most frequently, one with ə. The problem is to know when and where to use the various forms, and to get into the way of using them.

Weak forms

The words we are here concerned with include most of the commonest words in the English language. They have more than one pronunciation: the one they would be given if used in their 'citation form', i.e. in isolation (which hardly ever happens), also whenever they carry strong stress in context, and in certain other cases even without strong stress; this is known as the strong form. They also have one or more other pronunciations which are the ones used the greater part of the time in ordinary conversation and in other situations when the language is spoken connectedly; and these are called their weak forms.

Weak forms have several possible features: some drop a consonant, others drop a vowel, as compared to the strong form of the words; most show a difference of vowel and of these the majority have ə where the strong form has some other vowel. The following table shows words whose weak form (or one of them) has ə, arranged according to the vowel sound of their strong form:

i	ɛ	æ	ɑ	ɒ	ɔ	ʊ	ʌ	ɜ	ɪɜ	ɛə
the	*them*	*am*	*are*	*from*	*for*	*do*	*but*	*her*	*a*	*there*
		an		*of*		*to*	*does*	*were*		
		and		*was*			*must*			
		as					*some*			
		can					*us*			
		had								
		has								
		have								
		than								
		that								

Some of the above have additional weak forms with a consonant less, or a vowel less, or both. For example, the word *and* has strong form ænd, with weak forms ənd, ən, nd, n, each of which has its proper uses. Clearly, such differences cannot as a rule be shown in ordinary spelling, though a few reduced or contracted forms can, with the help of an apostrophe, as in *I'll, he'd, you've*. But writers of dialogue often spell out the full forms in cases where a contraction would in fact be spoken, so the orthography is of little help even here. Notice that in no case of ə being pronounced does the orthography give any indication of this. There would be little point even supposing it had the means and attempted to do so, for the choice between strong and weak form is quite often optional, varying between speakers, and from one moment to the next with the same speaker, depending on speaking rate, position in the sentence of the word in question, and other factors. Besides, since some words have several weak forms that might be used, no *one* spelling would cover them all. Native English-speakers naturally make a choice between suitable forms unconsciously as they speak; this the foreign learner obviously cannot do, but he must also expect in any case to have considerable difficulty in learning the usage, partly because ordinary spelling can give no guidance – and is in fact actively misleading – and partly because the phenomenon of weakening and the occurrence of a central vowel quality may be unknown to him from his mother tongue.

Only indifferent results can be expected from exhorting the learner to observe the usage of English people as they speak – though this, to be sure, is the advice one would give to the advanced student. For connected material, phonetically transcribed texts are very valuable: they of course show the distribution of all sounds in all words, but they greatly facilitate study of the incidence of shwa in spoken English. But even if, in a given teaching situation, a full set of phonetic symbols is not to be used, a superscript ə over orthography has much to commend it, just for this special purpose. To show how this works out in practice, and to make clear the extent of the problem, a short specimen text is given below, one version orthographic with ə superscripts, the other in full phonetic notation (see pp. 91–2 for Tables of the symbols used). The passage contains a total of 160 syllables, of which 32 contain ə (20%) including 17 weak forms (10%).

A: Have you read *Southᵊern Ádvᵊentureᵊ?*

B: No, but I read ᵊa revᵊiew ofᵊit the othᵊer day. It said it wᵊas very good. Let me see, it's by Patrick Burton, isn't it?

A: Er...no, Patrick *Buxᵊton.* You're probᵊably thinking ofᵊ *Philip* Burton. You know, theᵊ man who wrote *Undᵊer theᵊ Weathᵊer.*

B: Oh yes! I always mix those two up. But it *is* the book I read abᵊout in the article, I'm sure. It's ᵊabout somᵊe people who go off tᵊo South Aᵊmerica, isn't it, ᵊand they get involved in all sorts ofᵊ mad aᵊdventures?

A: Yes, that's right. It's extremely well written, ᵊand most aᵊmusing in parts.

B: I *must* read it. I'll see if I caᵊn get Dick tᵊo give it me fᵊor my birthday.

A: 'hæv ju rɛd 'sʌðən əd'vɛntʃə ?

B: 'nəʊ, bət ʌɪ 'rɛd ə rɪ'vju əv ɪt ðɪ 'ʌðə 'dɛɪ. ɪt 'sɛd ɪt wəz 'vɛrɪ 'gʊd. 'lɛt mi 'si, ɪt s bʌɪ 'pætrɪk 'bɜtn, 'ɪznt ɪt ?

A: ɜ . . . 'nəʊ, pætrɪk 'bʌkstən. jɔ 'prɒbəblɪ 'θɪŋkɪŋ əv 'fɪlɪp bɜtn. 'ju 'nəʊ, ðə 'mæn hu rəʊt 'ʌndə ðə 'wɛðə.

B: 'əʊ 'jɛs. ʌɪ 'ɔlwɛɪz mɪks 'ðəʊz tu 'ʌp. bət ɪ'tɪz ðə bʊk ʌɪ 'rɛd əbʌʊt ɪn ðɪ 'ɑtɪkl, ʌɪ m 'ʃɔ. ɪt s əbʌʊt səm 'pipl hu gəʊ 'ɒf tə 'sʌʊθ ə'mɛrɪkə, 'ɪznt ɪt, ən ðɛɪ gɛt ɪn'vɒlvd ɪn 'ɔl 'sɔts əv 'mæd əd'vɛntʃəz ?

A: 'jɛs, 'ðæt s 'rʌɪt. ɪt s ɪks'trimlɪ 'wɛl 'rɪtn, ən 'məʊst ə'mjuzɪŋ ɪn 'pɑts.

B: ʌɪ 'mʌst rid ɪt. ʌɪ l 'si ɪf ʌɪ kən gɛt 'dɪk tə 'gɪv ɪt mi fə mʌɪ 'bɜθdɛɪ.

Now as regards how to go about the teaching of weak forms, advice to the teacher must be: to face the problem and begin to tackle it from the outset. Admittedly, the strong form of a word has to be uttered when it is first introduced and spoken in isolation. This will be the 'citation form' referred to on p. 74. But in the very next breath, as it were, and as soon as the word is incorporated in the simplest phrase, it should be pronounced by the teacher with the weak form that would be appropriate; attention should be drawn to the *difference* between the isolated word, the strong form, and the weak form of the word as it sounds in the particular sentence; and the correct form should be insisted upon from the start and anything else rejected as unsuitable in the context.

Natural slowness of articulation may induce strong forms in the speech of the elementary foreign learner – as it tends to do in that of native speakers themselves. But this should be tolerated only for the first few minutes: as soon as the phrase can be uttered fluently – which should be the aim in any event – the proper weak forms should be elicited. Otherwise the pernicious habit sets in of merely saying the strong forms, wherever they occur in a sentence, faster and faster – the universal tendency of generations of foreign speakers of English!

A special word to the teacher who wishes to demonstrate slowly and clearly whatever English phrase is to be learnt: considerable skill is needed to maintain the desirable weak forms in the pronunciation as soon as the rate of speaking is reduced below that of a normal conversational style. If the rate of delivery is *too* slow, the use of weak forms would of course be unnatural, and their artificial demonstration at very slow tempo (or in isolation) can be looked upon as being in the province of the expert. A suitable compromise must be found: even for a first presentation of the material, the speaking rate adopted should never be so slow that connected speech must disintegrate – giving rise not only to strong forms but to breaks in what should be continuous, to glottal stops, incorrect intonation and a host of other undesirable features. Rather than this, the tempo of even a first presentation should always be such as will sound natural – weak forms and all. But a teacher needs to cultivate assiduously the control of breath and articulation that will make this possible, and above all to be aware of what to aim at and what to avoid.

There follow a number of short phrases exemplifying some of the most frequently occurring weak forms with ə, arranged in alphabetical order of the ordinary spelling of the words. These could be used for rehearsal as they stand, or they may suggest to the teacher different examples perhaps better suited, as regards vocabulary or structures, to the stage his pupils have reached in their studies.

Weak form practice

The phrases are set out below in ordinary spelling and again, phonetically transcribed, on the page opposite.

A

such a pity
what a joke
not a lot
to have a bath
we'll find a way
I took a chance

AM

what am I doing?
where am I to go?
how am I to know?

AND

egg and bacon
well and good
black and white
hale and hearty

ARE, ARE THE

when are they coming?
what are you doing?
why are you laughing?
how are you getting on?

these are the best
those are the ones
mine are the biggest

AS, AS . . . AS

just as you like
rather as I thought
come as my guest

as far as I know
as easy as anything
as good as gold
as hard as nails

AS A, AS THE

not as a rule
only as a joke
dressed as a man

just as the bell rang
just as the train left

AT, AT A, AT THE

not at home
all at once
not at present
look at that

one at a time

knock at the door
just at the moment

BUT, BUT A, BUT THE

last but one
tired but happy
all but Mary

nothing but a sham
all but a few

nothing but the best
all but the youngest

CAN, CAN THE

you can take it
we can have them
if you can manage
I can ask him
three can play

what can the matter be?
how can the thing work?

A

'sʌtʃ ə 'pɪtɪ
'wɒt ə 'dʒəʊk
'nɒt ə 'lɒt
tə 'hæv ə 'baθ
wi l 'fʌɪnd ə 'wɛɪ
ʌɪ 'tʊk ə 'tʃans

AM

'wɒt əm ʌɪ 'duɪŋ
'wɛər əm ʌɪ tə 'gəʊ
'hʌʊ əm ʌɪ tə 'nəʊ

AND

'ɛg ən 'bɛɪkən
'wɛl ən 'gʊd
'blæk ən 'wʌɪt
'hɛɪl ən 'hatɪ

ARE, ARE THE

'wɛn ə ðɛɪ 'kʌmɪŋ
'wɒt ə ju 'duɪŋ
'wʌɪ ə ju 'lafɪŋ
'hʌʊ ə ju 'gɛtɪŋ 'ɒn

'ðiz ə ðə 'bɛst
'ðəʊz ə ðə 'wʌnz
'mʌɪn ə ðə 'bɪgɪst

AS, AS . . . AS

'dʒʌst əz ju 'lʌɪk
'raðər əz ʌɪ 'θɒt
'kʌm əz mʌɪ 'gɛst

əz 'far əz ʌɪ 'nəʊ
əz 'iz əz 'ɛnɪθɪŋ
əz 'gʊd əz 'gəʊld
əz 'had əz 'nɛɪlz

AS A, AS THE

'nɒt əz ə 'rul
'əʊnlɪ əz ə 'dʒəʊk
'drɛst əz ə 'mæn

'dʒʌst əz ðə 'bɛl ræŋ
'dʒʌst əz ðə 'trɛɪn 'lɛft

AT, AT A, AT THE

'nɒt ət 'həʊm
'ɔl ət 'wʌns
'nɒt ət 'prɛznt
'lʊk ət 'ðæt

'wʌn ət ə 'tʌɪm

'nɒk ət ðə 'dɔ
'dʒʌst ət ðə 'məʊmənt

BUT, BUT A, BUT THE

'last bət 'wʌn
'tʌɪəd bət 'hæpɪ
'ɔl bət 'mɛərɪ

'nʌθɪŋ bət ə 'ʃæm
'ɔl bət ə 'fju

'nʌθɪŋ bət ðə 'bɛst
'ɔl bət ðə 'jʌŋgɪst

CAN, CAN THE

ju kən 'tɛɪk ɪt
wi kən 'hæv ðəm
'ɪf ju kən 'mænɪdʒ
ʌɪ kən 'ask hɪm
'θri kən plɛɪ

'wɒt kən ðə 'mætə bi
'hʌʊ kən ðə θɪŋ 'wɜk

FOR, FOR A, FOR THE

not for long
wait for Tom
tea for two
ask for more

ring for a taxi
longing for a drink
looking for a place
going for a walk

all for the best
ring for the doctor
good for the teeth
not for the moment

FROM, FROM A, FROM THE

far from well
take it from me

seen from a train
a letter from a friend
reading from a book

I got it from the shelf
one from the back
two from the front

OF, OF A, OF THE

out of doors
the best of luck
a lot of nonsense
a block of flats
that kind of thing
Master of Arts

out of a bottle

the rest of the news
the side of the road
the end of the story
the start of the trouble

THAT, THAT A, THAT ARE, THAT THE

now that we're alone
I know that I'm right

all that a man could want

the ones that are mine
those that are here

now that the rain has stopped

TO, TO . . . TO, TO THE

we want to go
you ought to do it
I'd like to see
first to speak
last to leave

to take to bits
to go to town
to go to pieces
do get to the point
this way to the station

WAS, WAS A, WAS THE

what was that?
who was first?
how was I to know?
what was I saying?

that was a mistake

John was the best
Mary was the last
which was the largest?

WERE, WERE A, WERE THE

what were you saying?
where were they going?

you were a fool

those were the best

80

FOR, FOR A, FOR THE

'nɒt fə 'lɒŋ
'weɪt fə 'tɒm
'ti fə 'tu
'ask fə 'mɔ

'rɪŋ fər ə 'tæksɪ
'lɒŋɪŋ fər ə 'drɪŋk
'lʊkɪŋ fər ə 'pleɪs
'gəʊɪŋ fər ə 'wɔk

'ɔl fə ðə 'bɛst
'rɪŋ fə ðə 'dɒktə
'gʊd fə ðə 'tiθ
'nɒt fə ðə 'məʊmənt

FROM, FROM A, FROM THE

'fa frəm 'wɛl
'tɛɪk ɪt frəm 'mi

'sɪn frəm ə 'trɛɪn
ə 'lɛtə frəm ə 'frɛnd
'rɪdɪŋ frəm ə 'bʊk

ʌɪ 'gɒt ɪt frəm ðə 'ʃɛlf
'wʌn frəm ðə 'bæk
'tu frəm ðə 'frʌnt

OF, OF A, OF THE

'ʌʊt əv 'dɔz
ðə 'bɛst əv 'lʌk
ə 'lɒt əv 'nɒnsns
ə 'blɒk əv 'flæts
'ðæt kʌɪnd əv θɪŋ
'mɑstər əv 'ɑts

'ʌʊt əv ə 'bɒtl

ðə 'rɛst əv ðə 'njuz
ðə 'sʌɪd əv ðə 'rəʊd
ðɪ 'ɛnd əv ðə 'stɔrɪ
ðə 'stɑt əv ðə 'trʌbl

THAT, THAT A, THAT ARE, THAT THE

'nʌʊ ðət wɪər ə'ləʊn
ʌɪ 'nəʊ ðət ʌɪ m 'rʌɪt

'ɔl ðət ə 'mæn kʊd 'wɒnt

ðə 'wʌnz ðət ə 'mʌɪn
'ðəʊz ðət ə 'hɪə

'nʌʊ ðət ðə 'rɛɪn əz 'stɒpt

TO, TO . . . TO, TO THE

wi 'wɒnt tə 'gəʊ
ju 'ɔt tə 'du ɪt
ʌɪ d 'lʌɪk tə 'si
'fɑst tə 'spik
'lɑst tə 'liv
tə 'tɛɪk tə 'bɪts
tə 'gəʊ tə 'tʌʊn
tə 'gəʊ tə 'pisɪz

'du 'gɛt tə ðə 'pɒɪnt
'ðɪs 'wɛɪ tə ðə 'stɛɪʃn

WAS, WAS A, WAS THE

'wɒt wəz 'ðæt
'hu wəz 'fɜst
'hʌʊ wəz 'ʌɪ tə 'nəʊ
'wɒt wəz ʌɪ 'sɛɪɪŋ
'ðæt wəz ə mɪs'tɛɪk

'dʒɒn wəz ðə 'bɛst
'mɛərɪ wəz ðə 'lɑst
'wɪtʃ wəz ðə 'lɑdʒɪst

WERE, WERE A, WERE THE

'wɒt wə ju 'sɛɪɪŋ
'wɛə wə ðeɪ 'gəʊɪŋ

ju wər ə 'ful

'ðəʊz wə ðə 'bɛst

4.4   Activity at the larynx

The complex physiological movements within the larynx can be divided, for the purposes of the foreign language learner, into two basically different activities: the vibration and the non-vibration of the vocal cords, known as voicing or 'voice' and 'breath' respectively. The complication is in the *timing* of these two activities relative to other things going on at the same instant, and here there are marked differences between languages. Wherever such differences in speech behaviour exist, there will be found problems for the learner of a foreign language.

Unvoicing

In English there is a tendency for vocal cord vibration to start up a fraction late when certain consonant articulations requiring voicing are about to begin. This delayed onset of voicing is termed 'unvoicing' in two cases: where the consonant in question is initial after a pause or silence, and where the consonant in question has been preceded by another, *voiceless* consonant articulation. (See Aspiration, on next page, for another case of delayed onset of voicing.)

There is also a tendency in English for vocal cord vibration to die away during a voiced consonant articulation and to stop altogether before the breath for the consonant has ceased to flow; this early cessation of vocal cord vibration is also termed unvoicing, and is evident in two cases: where the consonant in question is final in its group and therefore followed by silence, and where the consonant is followed by another, *voiceless* consonant articulation.

Some typical instances of unvoicing in English are represented diagrammatically below, where the horizontal line shows a sequence of events on a time track moving from left to right. The line is straight ————— when the vocal cords are not in vibration, wavy ∿∿∿∿∿when they are.

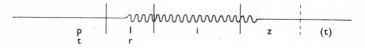

In the above words *please* and *trees* the consonants l r and z all show unvoicing, l and r during their earlier portion, z during its latter portion. In the phrase *please take*, unvoicing of z (before t) would be similar.

The amount of unvoicing, i.e. the proportion of time during which the articulation is voiceless in relation to its total duration, varies greatly from one individual to another and from one moment of speaking to the next, but it is often quite noticeable; those whose languages do not have this feature should note the relevant differences with English and, particularly with final 'voiced' plosives and fricatives, pay attention to the extremely *weak breath force* used for these sounds. This, rather than the presence of voicing during the articulation, is what to the English ear distinguishes the voiced from the corresponding voiceless sounds (together with aspiration of the voiceless plosives, see below). Thus to make the distinction between, for example, Eng. *cart* and *card*, or *calf* and *carve*, such weak breath force is used for the final consonant of *card* and *carve* that the sound is practically inaudible. (The longer vowel, as compared to that of *cart* and *calf*, is the other clue that the English hearer gets as to which of two words is being said.)

Aspiration

A further instance of delayed onset of vibration of the vocal cords is when a voiceless plosive (p t k) is followed at once by a vowel, especially in a syllable bearing strong stress: between the release of the plosive and the voicing for whatever vowel follows, a brief but perceptible emission of breath (voiceless air) intervenes; this is known as aspiration.

Points to note are: that aspiration is very slight and often negligible when the syllable to be uttered bears weak stress only; that no aspiration is present when s precedes the plosive, i.e. following the groups sp st sk; and that aspiration is lacking altogether in the speech of a certain number of native English-speakers.

Learners whose languages exhibit no aspiration can be encouraged to aim for a more 'English' effect by making as if to sound h immediately following the release of the plosive. So for saying *part* they should be told to release p and then pronounce *heart*; similarly to pronounce *tide* as *hide* after the release of t, and *coast* as *host* after a released k.

Pitch variation

Variation in pitch results from variation in the frequency of vibration of the vocal cords, which are situated inside the larynx and form part of it. The vocal cords can be adjusted in the airstream so as to open and shut regularly (to 'vibrate'); this they can do within a range of speeds between roughly a hundred and a thousand times per second, thus producing in the hearing receiver the sensation of a lower or a higher musical note or pitch. Intonation in language is the rise and fall of voice pitch over a stretch of speech, and an analysis of the intonation of a language seeks to establish what kinds of pitch variation can occur and under what circumstances.

There are no remarks that can usefully be made on the subject of the intonation of English in particular, which would be of assistance to the foreign learner wanting to manage the rise and fall of his own voice in suitable ways, or to the teacher wishing to be helpful to his pupils in this area. Whether or not the topic of intonation is tackled independently for its own sake – and in many situations the decision to treat it only *incidentally* may be the best one – there are two general points to be borne in mind: the learner should not be allowed to carry over into the target language patterns or habits of intonation that belong in his own language but sound strange or incorrect elsewhere; and he should be helped to manage the rise and fall of his voice in any ways that are characteristic of the target language but not found in his own.

Directing the learner's attention, however simply, to intonational phenomena in their own right is the first necessary step, followed by giving him practice in deciding for himself whether one feature or another is or is not present in the graded utterances that are then submitted orally for his consideration and assessment. He should next be given practice in recognising these features in actual language material, in order to connect the intonation itself with the type of sentence (statement, question), with the attitude conveyed by the speaker (emphasis, disinterestedness) which is superimposed on the actual form of words, and with the situational context in which the exchange of words is, or is imagined to be, taking place. After plenty of this kind of work, the learner is in a better position to monitor his own speech as he tries to reproduce the various effects in accordance with the usages he has been studying.

A word of reassurance may be added at this point: English-speakers themselves do not all conform to the same patterns of rise and fall or to an identical use of the patterns. So any statements on intonation must remain largely generalisations, and a foreign speaker who departs from one usage may well be conforming to another that is regionally or even just personally different. It is flexibility in execution that should be cultivated, in order that a particular effect can be conveyed *if desired*. And above all, sensitivity to the operation of pitch variation is needed so that native subtleties of meaning or attitude should not be lost on the foreign listener, and in order that the non-native language user may not unwittingly convey some wrong impression as he speaks. Needless to say, these remarks are made with the more advanced learner in mind.

Intonation in English is intimately bound up with the incidence of strong stresses: a speaker uncertain of where in a sentence to put strong stress can hardly expect to hit upon a suitable intonation. Conversely, however, correct placing of strong stresses cannot ensure correct intonation since a *choice* of intonation patterns is so often available on any given succession of strong stresses. The teacher should point out that, though stress and intonation are different things, in practice they operate in conjunction; and in trying to obtain a satisfactory result from a learner, he should be ready to take quick decisions, based on his judgment of the pupil's needs, as to whether to attend to aspects of stress or of intonation.

4.5 Tongue activity

For all new, unfamiliar articulations the speech organs have to be trained to get into unaccustomed positions and perform unusual actions. A teacher, who needs to know just what is required in each case, can often obtain from books the information he wants (see Bibliography, p. 98). If it is not available in this form, he should do his best to get at the facts by asking other people or, better still, by noticing things for himself. When it comes to teaching a new articulation to his students, he should put into operation whatever methods he finds or expects to find successful (see pp. 26–8 for some teaching techniques and procedures).

Consonant combinations

Speakers of languages having few consonants articulated in succession find difficulty in coping with some of the English consonant clusters that can occur in the body of a word, or with agglomerations of consonants resulting from juxtaposition of words in connected speech. Thus initial **sp st sk** tend to have a vowel inserted *between* them by speakers of certain languages; others are inclined to *precede* the group by a vowel: Spanish-speakers have to learn not to say **estopit** for *stop it* (compare Sp. *España* – or Turkish *İspanya* – with Eng. *Spain*). Italians are as a rule able to articulate English groups quite easily, yet they have to inhibit a tendency to insert a vowel, of indeterminate or **a**-quality, after many a final consonant before a consonant beginning the next word, saying for instance **mɛkami** for *make me*.

Each of the above types of mispronunciation or pronunciation difficulty arises directly from the phonology of the language referred to: thus in Italian most syllables are open and nearly all *final* syllables are open; this means that every Italian word is likely to end with a vowel, so it really 'goes against the grain' of Italian phonology, and the habits of speech acquired from it, *not* to follow a consonant with a vowel, especially at word endings – hence the unwanted vowel that Italian speakers are inclined to insert when speaking English.

Whatever the exact nature of the articulatory problem may be, the general procedure for overcoming it will be the same: to rehearse the troublesome sequence first *slowly enough to get the succession of movements right*, and then with gradually increasing speed until greater facility has been gained. A speaker can always develop skill greater than he already possesses – simply by further practice.

A teacher should always let learners know in which cases combinations of consonants are liable to be reduced or simplified *even by native speakers*, otherwise they may go out of their way to pronounce conscientiously a number of adjacent consonants when in fact one or more – perhaps in the middle of the group – would normally not be pronounced at all. Each language has its own way of simplifying sequences of articulations, and fluency and naturalness are promoted by assisting a learner to incorporate these tendencies into his speaking of the target language. (See Assimilation, Elision in Glossary.)

4.6 Facial movement

English is spoken with comparatively little movement of the mouth and jaw and with relatively less tension of the articulatory muscles generally than in the case of many other languages. Speakers of such languages should therefore cultivate pronouncing English with *less vigorous* activity than normal for them and should deliberately aim for a degree of relaxation with the intention of counteracting that *extra* effort that all tend to make when learning to perform and co-ordinate the unfamiliar movements of a foreign language. A general indistinctness of speech is hardly to be recommended but, provided quite strong breath force is expended on the appropriate (strongly stressed) syllables, there is much to be said for cultivating something of a 'mumble' – but on condition that this extends only to certain phonetic features, namely the reduction of unimportant syllables by omission of certain consonants, by a more rapid articulation of these syllables, with central vowel qualities as required, and a slackening of muscular tension in their articulation generally.

Less facial movement is noticeable in connection with any rounding and protrusion of the lips. There are three points about lip-rounding in English: first, there are proportionately rather fewer vowels in the English system that have any lip-rounding at all; second, the statistical frequency of occurrence of such vowels in connected speech is low; and third, the lip-rounding, when there is any, is rather slight, so that the corners of the mouth are not drawn together very firmly and the lips are not much protruded. Any tendency of the foreign speaker to make *excessive* mouth movement can therefore usefully receive comment from the teacher.

Diphthongs

One case where *more* movement is involved in English than in some other languages is in the pronunciation of diphthongs, because here a deliberate change of position of the articulating organs is called for during the production of a vowel sound in a single syllable.

Many languages have no diphthongs, and although some of the English diphthongs can easily be learnt just from imitation – since there is no particular difficulty in gliding from one vowel quality towards another, and many languages have juxtaposed vowels in *successive* syllables – nevertheless there is a widespread tendency to replace certain English diphthongs by monophthongs. It should however be noted that varieties of English exist with just these characteristics, e.g. Scottish English, so when for example speakers of Indian languages or of Arabic, among many others, pronounce in such a manner, this could hardly count as 'wrong', nor would this way of speaking be likely in itself to cause difficulty in understanding. What one can say is that a foreign speaker is more likely to draw attention to the fact of his foreignness (which may of course be obvious anyhow) than to be identified by native English-speakers as having, for instance, learnt his English in Scotland or from Scots.

A decision therefore has to be reached as to what variety of English to take as a model, and whether to insist on diphthongs for the vowels in Eng. *day* and *go*, aiming for ɛɪ and əʊ rather than e and o. Provided these vowels are made rather long in any case, no confusion is likely to result; the important thing is to keep them apart from other vowels in the system, maintaining a distinction in ɛɪ (or e) as opposed to short ɛ (as in *laid/led*, *gate/get*), and in əʊ (or o) as opposed to short ɒ (as in *dole/doll*, *road/rod*). N.B. əʊ (or o) must in any case be kept distinct from another *long* vowel in the system – ɔ (as in *whole/hall*, *coat/caught*).

The clue to teaching a diphthongal pronunciation, if this is decided upon, is to insist on starting from a *lowered* jaw position for ɛɪ and raising it smartly during the syllable; and to insist on starting from an *unrounded* mouth position for əʊ and rounding perceptibly during the sound.

4.7 Inventory of principal mispronunciations of English by speakers of other languages

(the letters after each item relate to the Categories described on pp. 31–2)

Common tendencies generally

1 Incorrect sounds and sequences of sounds due to influence of ordinary spelling, inconsistencies in English spelling, and unexpected values of some letters. **C/D**
2 Many vowels under weak stress not given central quality they should have, either because this quality unknown from mother tongue or because ordinary spelling gives no indication. **B/D**
3 Other r-sounds for Eng. r. **B**
4 r pronounced before a consonant and finally. **B/C**
5 Confusion of one vowel with another, due to large number of distinctions in operation in the English system. Pairs of vowels commonly confused or the second pronounced like the first: i/ɪ, ʌ/ɑ, ɒ/ʌ, ɛ/ɛɪ, ɔ/əʊ. **A**
6 Distribution of long/short vowels; inability to make long vowels long enough (Nos. 1, 5, 7, 9, 11, see p. 92); at a later stage, long vowels made too long before voiceless consonants. **B**
7 Eng. θ ð: replaced by t d; or by s z; or by f v. **A**
8 Eng. v/w. **A**
9 Incorrect placing of strong stress, due to variable position of stress in English words, and uncertainty over which words to bring out in a sentence. **B/D**
10 Too many strong forms in place of weak forms of words. **B**

Outstanding or additional tendencies or difficulties of speakers of 5 particular languages

French

1 Syllable-timing for stress-timing. **D**
2 Strong stresses misplaced. **C**
3 Omission of h. **B**
4 Too much voicing in final b d g v z ʒ. **B/D**
5 Lip-rounding for ʒ, ə. **B**

German

1 Insertion of glottal plosive before initial vowel in word or syllable. **B/C**

88

2 v for w, tʃ for dʒ, p t k f s ʃ for word-final b d g v z ʒ. **B(A)**
3 Excessive lip-rounding for ʃ tʃ. **E**
4 ɛ for Eng. æ (*man* pronounced like *men*, *bad* like *bed*). **A**
5 Eng. ɑ too front, Eng. ɪə ɛə too close (i.e. pronounced iə eə). **B/C**

Italian

1 Insertion of vowel to separate consonant clusters or after final consonant. **B**
2 Lengthening of penultimate vowel if strongly stressed, as in *never*, *sorry*. **C**

Russian

1 Word-final b d g v z ʒ replaced by p t k f s ʃ. **B(A)**
2 Vowel qualities in weakly stressed syllables (if not ə). **D**
3 l too dark ('hard' or velarised). **E**
4 x for h. **B**

Spanish

1 Substitution of x for h, s for ʃ. **B, A**
2 Difficulty with some consonant clusters. **B**
3 Uncertainty over distribution of d/ð, b/v, final m/n. **A**
4 Long vowels not long enough. **B**

Appendix

Diagram 1 The organs of speech

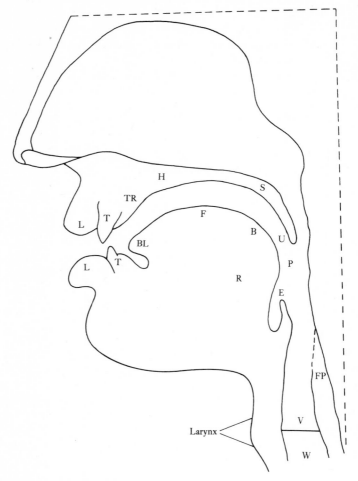

B	Back of tongue	BL	Blade of tongue	E	Epiglottis
F	Front of tongue	FP	Food passage	H	Hard palate
L	Lip	P	Pharynx	R	Root of tongue
S	Soft palate	T	Teeth	TR	Teeth ridge
U	Uvula	V	Position of vocal cords	W	Windpipe

Table 1 Phonetic Symbols occurring in the Text[1]

(stress is marked only when not on the first syllable)

a	Fr. *femme* fam	n	Eng. *now* nʌʊ
ai	Ger. *Bein* bain	ŋ	Eng. *sing* sɪŋ
a̠	It. *salata* sa̠'la̠ta̠	o	Fr. *beau* bo, Ger. *wo* vo
ɑ	Eng. *calm* kɑm	ø	Fr. *deux* dø, Ger. *Öl* øl
ɒ	Eng. *got* gɒt	ɔ	Eng. *saw* sɔ, Ger. *doch* dɔx
ɒɪ	Eng. *voice* vɒɪs	ɔ̈	Fr. *comme* kɔ̈m
æ	Eng. *cat* kæt, Ger. *Bär* bær	œ	Fr. *seul* sœl, Ger. *zwölf* tsvœlf
b	Eng. *baby* bɛɪbɪ	ɔi	Ger. *neun* nɔin
ç	Ger. *dich* dɪç	θ	Eng. *think* θɪŋk
d	Eng. *day* dɛɪ, Fr. *deux* dø	p	Eng. *pipe* pʌɪp
ð	Eng. *then* ðɛn	r	Eng. *red* rɛd, Fr. *reine* rɛn,
e	Fr. *thé* te, Ger. *Tee* te		It. *ricco* rikko
ɛ	Eng. *red* rɛd, Fr. *chaise* ʃɛz	s	Eng. *since* sɪns
ɛɪ	Eng. *day* dɛɪ	ʃ	Eng. *ship* ʃɪp, Fr. *chez* ʃe
ɛə	Eng. *there* ðɛə	t	Eng. *take* tɛɪk, Fr. *tout* tu
ə	Eng. *about* ə'bʌʊt,	u	Eng. *move* muv, Fr. *doux* du
	Ger. *bitte* bɪtə	u̠	Ger. *gut* gu̠t
əʊ	Eng. *go* gəʊ	ʊ	Eng. *look* lʊk, Ger. *und* ʊnt
ə̠	Fr. *peser* pə̠ze	ʊə	Eng. *tour* tʊə
ɜ	Eng. *turn* tɜn	v	Eng. *voice* vɒɪs
g	Eng. *give* gɪv	ʌ	Eng. *luck* lʌk
h	Eng. *hand* hænd	ʌɪ	Eng. *die* dʌɪ
i	Eng. *see* si	ʌʊ	Eng. *now* nʌʊ
i̠	Fr. *qui* ki̠, Ger. *wie* vi̠	w	Eng. *went* wɛnt
ɪ	Eng. *give* gɪv, Ger. *Kind* kɪnt	x	Ger. *doch* dɔx
ɪə	Eng. *here* hɪə	y	Fr. *tu* ty, Ger. *kühl* kyl
ɨ	Rus. *сын* sɨn,	ʏ	Ger. *Hütte* hʏtə
	Rom. *cînd* kɨnd	ɥ	Fr. *lui* lɥi̠
j	Eng. *yet* jɛt	z	Eng. *zone* zəʊn
k	Eng. *come* kʌm	ʒ	Eng. *measure* mɛʒə,
l	Eng. *little* lɪtl		Fr. *jaune* ʒon
m	Eng. *may* mɛɪ		

[1] All phonetic symbols shown in this book come from the International Phonetic Alphabet, a 'modified roman' form of notation, i.e. based on the roman alphabet, with modifications and additions in accordance with recommended conventions as to use. Further conventions adopted from the I.P.A. for this book are the use of a raised (or lowered) vertical mark preceding a syllable to indicate a strong (or secondary strong) stress falling on it; and the printing of a symbol in italics to indicate optional non-pronunciation of a sound in the context shown.

Table 2 Some vowel notations for English

Vowel No.	Keyword	I	II	III	IV	V	VI	VII	Keyword	Vowel No.
1	beat	iː	iː	ii	iː	i	i	i	beat	1
2	sit	i	i	i	ɪ	ɪ	ɪ	ɪ	sit	2
3	get	e	e	e	e	e	ɛ	ɛ	get	3
4	bag	æ	a	a	æ	æ	a	æ	bag	4
5	calm	ɑː	ɑː	aa	ɑː	ɑ	ɑ	ɑ	calm	5
6	long	ɔ	o	o	ɒ	o	ɒ	ɒ	long	6
7	saw	ɔː	oː	oo	ɔː	ɔ	ɔ	ɔ	saw	7
8	put	u	u	u	ʊ	ʊ	ɷ	ʊ	put	8
9	moon	uː	uː	uu	uː	u	u	u	moon	9
10	cup	ʌ	ʌ	ʌ	ʌ	ʌ	ʌ	ʌ	cup	10
11	bird	əː	əː	əə	ɜː	ɜ	ɜ	ɜ	bird	11
12	*a*bout	ə	ə	ə	ə	ə	ə	ə	*a*bout	12
13	day	ei	ei	ei	eɪ	eɪ	eɪ	ɛɪ	day	13
14	go	ou	ou	ou	əʊ	əʊ	oɷ	əʊ	go	14
15	high	ai	ai	ai	aɪ	ɑɪ	aɪ	ʌɪ	high	15
16	how	au	au	au	aʊ	aʊ	aɷ	ʌʊ	how	16
17	boy	ɔi	oi	oi	ɔɪ	ɔɪ	ɒɪ	ɒɪ	boy	17
18	here	iə	iə	iə { ei	ɪə	·ɪə	ɪə	ɪə	here	18
19	there	ɛə	eə	eə	ɛə	eə	ɛə	ɛə	there	19
20	four	ɔə	oə	oə					four	20
21	tour	uə	uə	uə	ʊə	ʊə	ɷə	ʊə	tour	21

I	II	III	IV	V	VI	VII	
11(ː)	7(ː)	7	14(ː)	12	14	12	Number of different letters in use.
6(ː)	2(ː)	2	10(ː)	8	9	10	Number of non-roman letters in use.
7	10	14	1	4	3	2	Number of English vowels shown by roman letters only.

Notation   I   II   III   IV   V   VI   VII

(see accompanying notes opposite)

Notes on the Vowel Notations

I   Became well known from Daniel Jones, *Outline of English Phonetics*, first published in 1918, and especially his *English Pronouncing Dictionary* (later *Everyman's*), first published in 1917. Has been used in many other books, including O'Connor, *Better English Pronunciation* and Hornby, *Advanced Learner's Dictionary*, pre-1974 editions. Three letters appear only in the diphthongs – a ɛ o.

II   A 'simplified' version of I above. First appeared in N. C. Scott, *English Conversation Reader* (1942).

III   A further simplification of I by doubling letters instead of using the colon (:) after a letter. First appeared in P. MacCarthy, *English Pronunciation* (1944), then in other books by the same author up to 1965 (*A Practice Book of English Speech*).

IV   First appeared in A. C. Gimson, *Introduction to the Pronunciation of English* (1962), then in several more works by the same author and by others. Each monophthong has a different letter, but two further letters appear only in diphthongs (a ɛ), while the roman letter o is not used.

V   First appeared in J. Windsor Lewis, *Concise Pronouncing Dictionary* (1972), and in the *Oxford Advanced Learner's Dictionary*, 1974 edition (Hornby). Each monophthong has a different letter and no other letters are added for the diphthongs. The roman letter a is not used (or could be used in place of ɑ).

VI   First appeared in D. Abercrombie, *English Phonetic Texts* (1964). Each monophthong has a different letter, but two more letters appear only in diphthongs (e o).

VII   First used for this book. Each monophthong has a different letter and no other letters are added for the diphthongs but every letter appearing in a diphthong stands for the vowel quality (within close limits) that it has when standing alone. The roman letters a e o are not used.

Remarks

    1 *No differences of pronunciation* are implied by any of the differences in the forms of notation: the same pronunciation is represented, differences are typographical only.

    2 Notations I, II and III show an extra diphthong (No. 20) but the other notations do not include it, as it is an inessential sound (speakers who do not have it use No. 7 instead in some words and No. 21 in others).

93

3 Notations II and III use roman letters as much as possible and manage with only two non-roman letters (ʌ ə). In Notation III nothing but roman letters are used for 14 of the 20/21 vowels; contrast Notation IV where only one vowel (e) is represented in roman letters.

4 Notations I, II and IV make use of a colon (:) in representing the five 'long' monophthongs. For Notations I and II the mark could not be omitted without causing visual confusion between vowels, but in Notation IV it could.

5 Comparison of Notations V, VI and VII reveals that seven of the monophthongs appear identically in all three notations (i ɑ ɔ u ʌ ɜ ə). Notation VII has six vowels as in V but not as in VI (ɪ æ ʊ əʊ ɪə ʊə), three vowels as in VI but not as in V (ɛ ɒ ɛə), and shows four diphthongs differently from either V or VI (ɛɪ ʌɪ ʌʊ ɒɪ), which also differ here from one another.

6 Only three letters ever appear with *different* values between notations:

  i stands for No. 1 in Notations V, VI and VII
      but for No. 2 in Notations I, II and III
  ɔ stands for No. 6 in Notation I
      but for No. 7 in Notations V, VI and VII
  u stands for No. 8 in Notations I, II and III
      but for No. 9 in Notations V, VI and VII

Diagram 2 English (RP) vowels

(for keywords see p. 92)

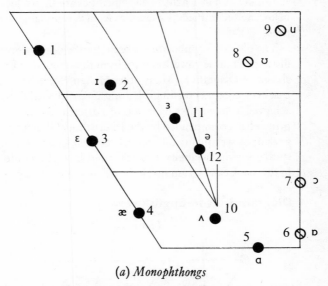

(*a*) *Monophthongs*

Filled dots stand for non-rounded, unfilled dots for rounded vowels

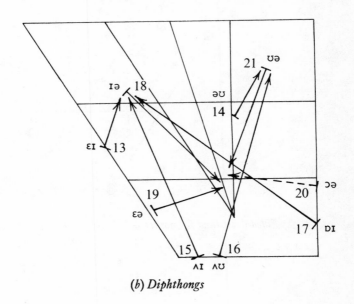

(*b*) *Diphthongs*

Some non-English vowels

A number of non-English vowel qualities are shown located on Diagram 3 below, and identified by examples from various languages, on the opposite page.

The phonetic symbols are chosen, for the purposes of this book, so as to distinguish these vowel qualities from those found in English (RP) and shown on Diagram 2. (Many other foreign vowels are not shown, e.g. nasal vowels, and non-English diphthongs.) Visual differentiation is achieved in some cases by means of a diacritical mark used according to principles recommended by the International Phonetic Association. As a result, vowel quality differences between languages, and between speakers within a language, that are *not* shown by a difference of notation in this book can be assumed to be slight and in most cases negligible.

Diagram 3 Non-English vowels

(for keywords see p. 97)

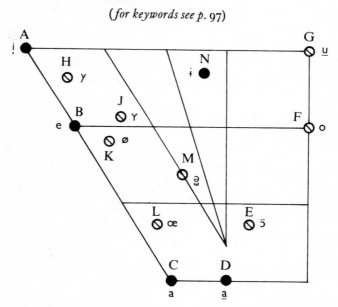

Filled dots stand for non-rounded, unfilled dots for rounded vowels

It is assumed, when not stated, that back vowels are rounded, front vowels not rounded. In French words, stress is not marked; in the other languages shown, stress is marked when not on the first syllable.

Vowel A i̥ very close, front. Fr. *dites* di̥t, Ger. *dies* di̥s.[1]

Vowel B e half close, front. Fr. *bébé* bebe, Ger. *geh* ge,[1] and very many other languages.

Vowel C a fully open, front. Parisian French *carte* kart, Hungarian *száz* saz.[1]

Vowel D a̠ open, retracted from front. It. *salata* sa̠'la̠ta̠,[2] Sp. *arma* a̠rma̠, and very many other languages.

Vowel E ɔ̈ half open, very centralised from back. Fr. *comme* kɔ̈m.

Vowel F o half close, back. Fr. *beau* bo, Ger. *so* zo.[1]

Vowel G u̠ close, very back. Ger. *gut* gu̠t.[1]

Vowel H y close front rounded. Fr. *vu* vy, Ger. *kühl* kyl.[1]

Vowel J ʏ half close rounded, very centralised from front. Ger. *Hütte* hʏtə.

Vowel K ø half close front rounded. Fr. *deux* dø, Ger. *Öl* øl.[1]

Vowel L œ half open front rounded. Fr. *seul* sœl, Ger. *Götter* gœtər.

Vowel M ɞ central rounded. Fr. *redoublement* rɞdublɞmã.

Vowel N ɨ close central unrounded. Turkish *sıkı* sɨ'kɨ, Romanian *cînd* kɨnd, Russian *сын* sɨn.

---

[1] As in the case of English, certain vowels of German, Hungarian and some other languages are always pronounced longer than the rest. When a vowel is adequately identified by its symbol, to mark the length separately would be redundant in the language concerned.

[2] In Italian a stressed vowel is lengthened in a non-final open syllable (i.e. when the vowel is followed by a single consonant, which will function as initial in the next, unstressed, syllable).

Bibliography

Manuals

Gimson, A. C. *An Introduction to the Pronunciation of English*. London: Edward Arnold, 1962.

Jones, Daniel. *An Outline of English Phonetics*. 9th edition. Cambridge University Press, 1975.

Kingdon, R. *The Groundwork of English Intonation*. London: Longmans, 1958.

The Groundwork of English Stress. London: Longmans, 1958.

MacCarthy, P. A. D. *English Pronunciation*. Cambridge: Heffer, 1944; last reprinted 1956.

O'Connor, J. D. *Better English Pronunciation*. Cambridge University Press, 1967. [with recordings]

O'Connor, J. D. and Arnold, G. F. *Intonation of Colloquial English*. London: Longmans, 1967. [with recordings]

Pring, J. T. *Colloquial English Pronunciation*. London: Longmans, 1959.

Schubiger, M. *English Intonation: its form and function*. Tübingen: Niemeyer, 1958.

Windsor Lewis, J. *A Guide to English Pronunciation*. Oslo: Scandinavian Universities Press, 1969.

MacCarthy, P. A. D. *The Pronunciation of French*. Oxford University Press, 1975. [with recording]

The Pronunciation of German. Oxford University Press, 1975. [with recording]

Pronouncing dictionaries

Jones, Daniel. *Everyman's English Pronouncing Dictionary*. 14th edition, extensively revised by A. C. Gimson. London: J. M. Dent and Sons, 1977.

Kenyon, J. S. and Knott, T. A. *A Pronouncing Dictionary of American English*. Springfield, Mass.: Merriam, 1944.

Miller, G. M. *BBC Pronouncing Dictionary of British Names*. Oxford
University Press, 1972.
Windsor Lewis, J. *A Concise Pronouncing Dictionary of British and
American English*. Oxford University Press, 1972.

Warnant, L. *Dictionnaire de la Prononciation française*. Gembloux,
Belgium: J. Duculot, 1962.
Krech, H. (ed.) *Wörterbuch der deutschen Aussprache*. Leipzig: VEB
Bibliographisches Institut, 1964.
Fiorelli, P., Migliorini, B. and Tagliavini, C. *Dizionario d'Ortografia e di
Pronunzia*. Turin: Edizioni RAI Radiotelevisione Italiana, 1969.

Phonetic readers

Abercrombie, D. *English Phonetic Texts*. London: Faber, 1964.
Arnold, G. F. and Gimson, A. C. *English Pronunciation Practice*.
University of London Press, 1965.
Lee, W. R. *An English Intonation Reader*. London: Macmillan, 1963.
MacCarthy, P. A. D. *English Conversation Reader*. London: Longmans,
1956.
O'Connor, J. D. *New Phonetic Readings*. Bern: Francke, 1948.
Advanced Phonetic Reader. Cambridge University Press, 1971. [with
recording]
Phonetic Drill Reader. Cambridge University Press, 1973. [with
recording]
Scott, N. C. *English Conversations*. Cambridge: Heffer, 1942 and 1965.
Tibbitts, E. L. *A Phonetic Reader for Foreign Learners of English*.
Cambridge: Heffer, 1958.

Practice materials

Gimson, A. C. *A Practical Course of English Pronunciation*. London:
Edward Arnold, 1975. [with recordings]
Kingdon, R. *English Intonation Practice*. London: Longmans, 1958.
MacCarthy, P. A. D. *A Practice Book of English Speech*. Oxford University
Press, 1965.
Mortimer, Colin. *Stress Time*. Cambridge University Press, 1976. [with
recording]
Clusters. Cambridge University Press, 1977. [with recording]
Contractions. Cambridge University Press, 1977. [with recording]
Link-up. Cambridge University Press, 1977. [with recording]
Weak Forms. Cambridge University Press, 1977. [with recording]

Tibbitts, E. L. *Practice Material for the English Sounds*. Cambridge: Heffer, 1963.

English Stress Patterns. Cambridge: Heffer, 1967.

Trim, J. L. M. *English Pronunciation Illustrated*. Cambridge University Press, 1965; 2nd edition, 1975. [with recordings]

Glossary

Articulation: the combination and co-ordination of movements, by the relevant parts of the vocal apparatus, for the production of a given linguistic sound.
To articulate: to pronounce.
Articulator: a part involved in an articulation.
'*Good articulation*': clear and definite movements of the articulators.

Aspiration: the delayed onset of vibration of the vocal cords following the release of a (usually) voiceless plosive, so that an emission of breath unaccompanied by voice precedes the voicing of the following vowel. (In some Indian languages, *voiced* plosives occur in which the release of the closure is followed by a greater flow of air than would suffice to keep the vocal cords in vibration. This creates a 'breathy' effect (termed 'aspiration') which may extend some way into the following vowel itself.)

Assimilation: the process by which the movements to articulate a sound are affected by those required for a neighbouring articulation. The resultant articulation is in some respect more similar to that neighbour than it would otherwise have been, or than it previously was. The phenomenon can be explained as due to the tendency to economise effort, to simplify and sometimes to anticipate. It may be observed in the historical development of a language, as when Latin *in* before *port-* gave *import*, *importance*, etc.; or during fluent speaking, as when It. *con te, con me* are pronounced kon te but kom me, or when Eng. *in case* is pronounced with a velar nasal, as for the *n* in *ink*. (See *Elision* for another type of simplification.)

Back vowel: a vowel sound articulated with the body of the tongue held towards the back of the mouth, with or without some degree of bunching up of the tongue. (See *Front vowel*.)

Central vowel: a vowel sound articulated with some degree of bunching up of the part of the body of the tongue intermediate between front and back. (See *Back vowel, Front vowel*.)

Centralisation: the process of moving the tongue, or the tendency to move the tongue, to a more central position in the mouth, as compared to one more back or more front, which it should occupy, or formerly occupied.

Cis-Atlantic: on this side of the Atlantic Ocean, when considered from the European side. (See *Trans-Atlantic*.)

Close vowel: a vowel sound articulated with the body of the tongue raised to near the roof of the mouth (hard or soft palate), but not so near to it as to cause perceptible friction to be produced when air is passed through the opening. (See *Open vowel*.)

Closed syllable: a syllable closed (checked) by a consonant following the syllabic nucleus (usually a vowel). A consonant at the end of a word always closes its syllable; a single consonant in the middle of a word usually opens (releases) the following syllable. Groups of two or more consonants in the middle of a word usually divide up, one or more closing the first syllable and one or more beginning the next. The precise way in which consonant groups divide varies with the language, and may be affected by the morphology (structure of the word). (See *Open syllable*.)

Co-articulation: the pronunciation of words in sequence, and the phenomena connected with transitions between articulations.

Consonant letter: a letter of the roman (or other) alphabet convention-ally and traditionally used to 'stand for' a consonant sound of the language – though it may possibly not represent a pronounced sound in a given word. Thus *p* and *l* are consonant letters which do not however represent sounds now pronounced in the English word *psalm*.

Consonant sound: a sound produced by an articulation involving some degree of constriction of the mouth passage. This includes constriction sufficient to produce audible friction at the point of narrowing, and also includes complete blocking of the passage. N.B. In books that deal with speech (including this book) the word 'consonant' always means 'consonant sound'. In everyday usage, the word 'consonant' often stands for 'consonant letter' (see *Consonant letter*). A technical term for 'consonant sound' is 'contoid'.

Diacritic: a small mark above, below or beside a letter but separate from it. In phonetic notation, diacritics are used to modify or qualify the value that a letter would otherwise indicate. In conventional orthographies, a certain number of accents (diacritics) are used in some languages to compensate for a shortage of separate letter shapes in the roman or other alphabet.

Digraph: (1) a letter shape constructed from a combination of two other letters, e.g. æ which is constructed from a and e; (2) a sequence of two letters which is used to 'stand for' a single sound, e.g. *sh* stands for ʃ in the English word *ship*.

Diphthong: a type of vowel sound having an audible change of quality, due to a movement of the articulating organs, during one and the same syllable. N.B. A glide from one vowel quality to another, heard during the transition from one vowel to another in successive (i.e. different) syllables, is therefore not a diphthong. In everyday usage, 'diphthong' is sometimes used for 'digraph' (see *Digraph*).
Diphthongisation: (1) a process involving the replacement of a steady vowel quality (see *Monophthong*) by one that changes; (2) a tendency to alter the quality of a vowel sound during its articulation (by making some movement of the articulating organs). N.B. Co-articulation sometimes produces effects amounting to diphthongisation (see *Co-articulation*).

Elision: the process by which a simplification in the movements to articulate a sequence of sounds results in the 'dropping', i.e. non-pronunciation of one of them, which is then said to be elided. The history of languages is full of instances of such reductions, but elisions may also occur during fluent speaking, resulting in shorter forms of some words when they occur in certain contexts, as when the *d* of Eng. *blind* is not sounded in saying *blind man*. (See *Assimilation* for another type of simplification.)

Frequency: the rate at which anything vibrates or oscillates, commonly expressed in cycles per second, i.e. the number of times the vibration or oscillation would take place if continued regularly for one second. The ear responds to frequency within a certain range, and is insensitive to frequencies outside this range. Within the range, a hearer perceives frequency in terms of a sensation of pitch, expressed as being on a higher or lower note according to the faster or slower rate of the original vibration. The human vocal cords can produce only frequencies within a narrower range than the overall audio-frequency range, with variation in the capability of individual voices. The normal speaking range is even narrower. (See *Pitch*.)

Fricative: a consonant produced with audible friction when the air is expelled through a narrowed air passage, e.g. f, v, s, z.

Front vowel: a vowel sound articulated with the body of the tongue held towards the front of the mouth, with or without some degree of bunching up of the tongue. (See *Back vowel*.)

Glottis: the space between the vocal folds (vocal cords). During normal breathing the glottis is open; when the vocal folds are drawn completely together the glottis is closed.

Intonation: the rise and fall of the voice in connected speech. To speak without intonation is to speak on a monotone. An analysis of the intonation of a speaker, or of a language, seeks to describe and codify the use of changes of voice pitch: some of these tie in with the structure of sentences and the flow of speech; some are 'attitudinal' and convey, whether consciously or involuntarily, the emotions and attitudes of the speaker. (See *Pitch*.)

Kinaesthetic: describes the sensation, or the awareness, of part of the body in motion relative to other parts. Kinaesthetic awareness of movement of the tongue in the mouth can be cultivated.

Larynx: the complicated mechanism in the throat incorporating the vocal folds that produce 'voice', and are also involved in coughing, together with the bony outer shell that protects the delicate parts inside. One corner of this outer structure, generally known as 'Adam's apple', can be seen protruding at the front of the neck. The whole of the larynx is raised during swallowing.

Logatom: a modern coinage on Greek roots, to mean word piece or wordlike sequence, i.e. the equivalent of meaningless or nonsense word. It has the merit as a technical term of appearing practically unchanged (unlike most words) whatever roman-scripted language a text is written in.

Minimal pair: a pair of words, of different meaning, that exist in a language, and that are minimally different in pronunciation. The difference may consist of a distinction of vowel, as in Eng. *pet* and *pat*, or of a distinction of consonant, as in Eng. *pat* and *hat* or *pat* and *pack*.

Monophthong: a type of vowel sound of unchanging quality (to all intents and purposes) over its whole length. In the case of many languages, all the vowels are monophthongs. (See *Diphthong*.)

Nucleus: (1) The nucleus of a syllable (or syllabic nucleus) is in most cases a vowel, but occasionally a consonant. It is the part of a syllable on which the main chest pulse falls, resulting commonly in the greatest prominence of sound. (2) The nucleus of an intonation group is the part of the tune where the most important pitch feature of the group occurs. As to which *is* the most important, this is bound up with the language concerned, and with the intonational features it contains.

Open syllable: a syllable in uttering which the flow of air during the syllabic sound that constitutes its nucleus (most usually a vowel) is not checked by a following consonant. An open syllable at the end of a word is checked instead by muscular action to reduce the flow, until the sound dies away. An open syllable in the body of a word is so called if a following consonant (most usually when it is a single one) belongs to a succeeding syllable by virtue of the pulse of that syllable occurring on or before the consonant and so incorporating it into its structure. (See *Closed syllable*.)

Open vowel: a vowel sound articulated with the body of the tongue low in the mouth. Normally the jaw angle and the mouth opening at the lips are also wide.

Orthography: the conventional, traditional spelling of a language. *Orthographic*: with reference to the ordinary spelling of a language, as opposed to any phonetic notation used to represent it.

Palatalisation: (1) the process of moving, or the tendency to move, the front of the body of the tongue to a more front position for articulating a sound; (2) in Russian, and some other languages, the simultaneous raising of the front of the body of the tongue during the articulation of a sound.

Parameter: the scale along which a single variable may vary. Thus, the parameter of pitch is the scale of differences in the rate of vibration of the vocal cords; the parameter of duration in language is the scale of differences of length that sounds may have. In a living spoken language a number of parameters are generally involved simultaneously.

Phoneme: those units (as heard or pronounced) of a spoken language that can be utilised to make differences between different words of the language. (N.B. There may be *no* difference between words of different meaning: then they are pronounced with the same sequence of phonemes.)

Phonemic: A phonemic notation or form of transcription of a language is one that is restricted to setting out its phonemes, i.e. other, non-phonemic features are excluded.

Phonemics: the study of the phonemes or phonemic system of languages.

Phonetic: (1) relating to the sound or sounds of a language. (2) A phonetic symbol is a letter or letter shape used to stand for a sound or sound feature of a language. (3) A phonetic spelling is a sequence of letters having a close correspondence to a sequence of sounds.

Phonetics: the subject dealing with the phenomena of spoken language. Phonetics is a branch of linguistics and, as a subject, can be considered to include sub-branches such as phonemics and phonology. In studying General Phonetics (i.e. Phonetics in general) it is possible to disregard phonemics and phonology, but it is hardly possible to consider the phonetics of a language without studying its phonology. (See *Phonology*.)

Phonology: the organisation and arrangement of the sounds of a spoken language considered as a system or set of systems; the study of this.

Phonological: with reference to the above. A phonological notation or form of transcription is one that sets forth aspects or features of the phonology of a language. This is not necessarily restricted to its phonemes, and indeed is not necessarily concerned with them.

Pitch: The human ear responds to frequencies within a certain range by conveying them to the brain and producing a sensation of tone which can be described as having a given pitch – high or low, steady or moving, according to the rate of vibration of the source of sound (fast or slow) and to its nature (constant or changing). Below a certain frequency all sensation of pitch is lost, and separate pulsations may be perceived in place of a musical note or sound. Above a certain frequency the ear is incapable of responding by conveying any sensation to the brain, and a 'sound' is then inaudible. The human voice is incapable of producing such low (slow rate) or such high (fast rate) frequencies as are not heard as a sound or musical note. Variations in pitch during speech create the rise and fall of the voice known as intonation. (See *Frequency*, *Intonation*.)

Plosive: a consonant produced when a complete closing of the air passage is followed by an audible release of the air compressed behind the closure, e.g. p, b, t, d, k, g.

Prominence: the fact of standing out auditorily. A number of factors can contribute to prominence, more than one being present at a time, as a rule. Prominence by loudness produced by breath force, prominence by some pitch feature (e.g. high pitch, moving pitch), prominence by greater duration – these are the principal factors. A sound or word or idea can also be made to stand out by being preceded by a short gap of silence.

Semantic: concerned with the meaning of words and phrases.
Semantics: the field of meaning in language; the study of this.

Shwa: the name of a letter of the Hebrew alphabet which has the characteristic of occurring only in syllables that do not and cannot bear strong stress. For this reason the term has been found suitable to refer to a vowel in other languages (e.g. English, French, German) that has the same feature. Other characteristics of shwa are that the vowel quality is indeterminate, neutral or central, and that the sound is often extremely short and lacking in prominence.

Stress: the amount of effort expended on a syllable. Stressed = with strong stress.
Stress-timing: the tendency for the strongly stressed syllables of an utterance to follow each other at regular, or more regular, intervals of time. (See *Syllable-timing*.)

Syllable: (1) A physiological syllable is that part of an utterance that is produced on one impulse of the breath, that is, with a single chest pulse. (2) An auditory syllable is an utterance that is judged to have a single peak of auditory prominence, i.e. two peaks of prominence constitute two auditory syllables. (3) An acoustic syllable is an utterance that shows a single electrical or other peak on an instrument for measuring such peaks. (4) A phonological syllable is that part of a word that can be separated from other parts in accordance with the structural 'rules' of the given language. N.B. It is comparatively easy to establish how many syllables are contained in an utterance; it is much more difficult, and sometimes impossible, to specify the point of division between syllables (other than phonological syllables, see (4) above).
Syllabic: (1) The syllabic nucleus is that part of a syllable which has the

greatest prominence and/or on which the greatest breath force is expended. (2) A syllabic consonant is one that has so much prominence, due to its carrying power and/or its duration, that it constitutes the nucleus of its syllable (otherwise the nucleus of a syllable is most usually a vowel).

Syllable-timing: the tendency for the syllables in a sequence of syllables to follow one another at equal, or more equal, intervals of time. (See *Stress-timing*.)

Syntax: the field of word order and arrangement.
Syntactic: concerned with the ordering and arrangement of words in forming sentences.

Target language: the language that is the object of study or acquisition.

Trans-Atlantic: on the other side of the Atlantic Ocean, when considered from the European side. (See *Cis-Atlantic*.)

Velarisation: the tendency to move the body of the tongue to a more back position, in the direction of the soft palate, during the articulation of a sound.

Vowel letter: a letter of the roman (or other) alphabet conventionally and traditionally used to 'stand for' a vowel sound of the language.

Vowel sound: a sound produced by an articulation having little or no constriction of the mouth passage, at least not enough to produce 'audible friction' during normal speaking. N.B. In books dealing with speech (including this one) the word 'vowel' always means 'vowel sound'. In everyday usage, the word 'vowel' often stands for 'vowel letter' (see *Vowel letter*). A technical term for 'vowel-like sound' is 'vocoid'.